The Rebel's Playbook
A How-To Guide for Resistance

by Lady Libertie

The Pamphleteer
an imprint of Imprintli Publishing

LIBRARY OF CONGRESS CATALOGING-IN-PUBLICATIONS DATA
Libertie, Lady.
The Rebel's Playbook: A How-To Guide for Resistance /
Lady Libertie
ISBN: 978-0-9894891-3-3
eISBN: 978-0-9894891-5-7
www.imprint.li

Book & Jacket design© Imprintli Publishing
v1.0

DEDICATION

For the women who refuse to be
silenced,
the rebels who fight in heels or
combat boots,
and the dreamers who see
freedom not as a luxury,
but as a birthright.

This is for every girl who has ever
been told to sit down and stay quiet,
and for every woman who stood
anyway.

May we persist, resist,
and never forget the power of our
collective roar.

Let's survive—and thrive—together.

Contents

4

Introduction: How to Use This Book

Advice and Stories from Women Who Have Been There, Done That

This isn't just a book—it's a call to action, a survival manual, and a tribute to the fierce women and girls who've defied authoritarian regimes with resilience, cunning, and courage. Inside these pages, you'll encounter incredible figures like **Agnes Chow**, the Hong Kong activist who became a symbol of democratic resistance, and **Maria Ressa**, the Filipino journalist who risked imprisonment to expose corruption and propaganda. Their stories remind us that standing up to oppression, no matter the cost, can spark movements that change the world.

Fascists are a reactionary force deployed by elites to crush revolution and maintain the status quo.

How To Lead a Resistance

We don't just do storytelling here, we're equipping you for action. Each chapter is packed with How-To strategies, checklists, and real-world advice to help you fight back effectively.

Learn how to recognize authoritarian propaganda before it takes hold, protect your privacy in a world of mass surveillance, and build coalitions that can withstand the forces of division and fear.

Whether you're organizing protests, resisting quietly in your community, or amplifying voices online, this book offers a pathway to resistance that's practical, powerful, and deeply human.

- In *"Stay Informed, Stay Fabulous,"* you'll discover how to navigate the disinformation minefield, identify trustworthy news sources, and use apps and tools to safeguard your digital footprint. From dodging propaganda traps to staying ahead of government surveillance, you'll find tips that are both accessible and actionable.
- In *"Allies Assemble,"* you'll learn how to forge broad coalitions that transcend differences, uniting communities in the fight against fascism. Because history teaches us that resistance is most effective when it's collective, and coalitions can amplify voices that would otherwise be drowned out.
- In *"Gaslighting Olympics,"* you'll read about activists like **Maria Ressa**, who has endured relentless online harassment, imprisonment, and censorship yet continues to fight for press freedom in the Philippines. Her story is paired with

a practical list of strategies for identifying and combating propaganda, ensuring you're not just informed but also ready to act.

Plus lots and lots of checklists!

- The Resistance Checklist
- Social media platforms that are safe
- Digital hygiene checklist
- Apps & tools for staying untrackable
- Advanced safety tactics
- Protecting your physical space
- Situational awareness
- Legal and financial protections
- How to build an emergency exit kit
- How to create a mutual aid network
- How to strengthen bonds and swap skills
- Avoiding burnout
- Setting boundaries
- Growing & sustaining a movement
- When to stay and fight and when to flee

Use this Book to Outwit, Outsmart, and Overcome

Fascism isn't just a relic of history. It's a threat we face today, whether it's through subtle erosion of rights or outright authoritarian rule. This book equips you to recognize the warning signs: leaders who thrive on division, regimes that control the flow of information, and policies designed to strip away individual freedoms under the guise of "security" or "order."

7

And the best part, this fight isn't about being perfect or fearless—it's about showing up, learning, and acting, even when fear feels overwhelming. It's about knowing that resistance doesn't have to look one way; it can be loud and public, quiet and strategic, or somewhere in between. Whether you're marching in the streets, creating art that defies oppression, or organizing behind the scenes, there's room for everyone in this fight.

So grab your pen, your protest sign, or your encryption app—because the fight for freedom starts here. Together, we'll dismantle the playbook of oppression and write a better future, one act of resistance at a time. Let's get to work.

Ready to turn the tables and fight back? Let's do this, and remember: resistance looks good on you.

What the heck is Fascism, anyway?

Fascism showed up in the early 20th century like a bad ex who just won't quit—angry, insecure, and ready to ruin the party. It latched onto the chaos after World War I, feeding off economic meltdowns, political drama, and the fear of big changes like socialism and democracy.

Lucky for us, it fired up some total badass revolutionaries!

Mussolini in Italy was the OG fascist, mixing nationalism, corporate power, and a whole lot of suppression to keep elites in charge.

Promising to bring the nation back to its "glory days", the whole deal was a toxic con. Instead of solutions, it blamed marginalized groups for society's problems, using fear and division to rally people under one harsh, controlling regime. Think of it as the ultimate gaslighting power grab.

LEON TROTSKY

Leon Trotsky

the revolutionary with the best glasses game in history, had *a lot* to say about fascism. He didn't just wave his arms around yelling "It's bad!" (though it was)–he dissected it like a scientist studying a dangerous virus. Lucky for us, his insights are still razor-sharp, and we're going to use them to arm ourselves for the fight ahead. So, grab a notebook and maybe a stiff drink, because class is in session.

Trotsky didn't sugarcoat it: Fascism is capitalism's ugly tantrum when it feels threatened. It's when the ruling elite, scared stiff by rising worker power or an angry underclass, turns to violence to maintain their grip on the system.

10

Fascism isn't just right-wing authoritarianism. It's a crisis in capitalism, where the ruling class uses violence and mass movements of angry, disillusioned people to crush opposition & tighten control.

What a Girl's Gotta Know

It's not a vibe shift; it's a whole system meltdown. And guess what? You're the collateral damage.

Trotsky vs. Fascism

Think of it like a rich kid flipping the Monopoly board when they're about to lose—except instead of game pieces flying, it's people's rights, lives, and freedoms. *A short history lesson*

Leon Trotsky wasn't just theorizing about fascism from a cozy armchair in some academic ivory tower—he was in the trenches, battling its rise in real time. Born Lev Davidovich Bronstein in 1879 in Ukraine, (yes, **that** Ukraine) Trotsky grew up in the chaos of a crumbling Russian Empire and became one of the most prominent leaders of the Bolshevik Revolution in 1917.

But the revolution that promised to smash the chains of capitalism didn't exactly go as planned. Trotsky wasn't just battling fascists; he was also locked in a life-and-death struggle with Stalin, his former revolutionary comrade turned nemesis. After Lenin's death in 1924, Stalin seized control of the Soviet Union, turning it into a totalitarian state.

Trotsky argued that Stalinism and fascism were two sides of the

12

same coin. Both used authoritarianism to crush dissent, consolidate power, and exploit workers. Stalin just wore a hammer and sickle instead of a swastika. Stalin didn't take criticism well. Trotsky was exiled in 1929, forced to wander the globe, from Turkey to France to Mexico, all while writing scathing critiques of Stalinism and fascism.

How Do You See it Coming?

Fascism Thrives on Hardship. It doesn't arrive overnight, it's a slow creep, like a bad houseguest who starts by overstaying their welcome and ends by setting your couch on fire.

When people feel hopeless about the economy or their place in society, they're more likely to fall for simplistic answers and strongman leaders.

Fascists thrive by exploiting fear and offering easy scapegoats for complex problems. In the U.S., this playbook has been used time and again, with immigrants, minorities, feminists, LGBTQ+ individuals, and progressives often painted as the villains. But when you dig a little deeper, you'll find the real causes of the crises that fascists love to exploit.

What To Watch For

Watch for leaders who attack independent courts, free press, and checks on their power. These are the warning flares.

13

Support independent institutions fiercely. Donate, volunteer, and make noise. A free press and fair courts are democracy's last defense.

Document everything. Fascists hate being exposed for their dirty work. Amplify evidence of their violence and show the world what's really happening.

Remember, the people peddling fascist narratives are often the ones responsible for the crises they blame on others. They're the Monopoly board-flippers, the ones hoarding the hotels while telling you to blame the guy with one railroad. Your job? Call them out, connect the dots, and refuse to let them get away with it.

Fascists hate nothing more than a well-informed, well-organized, and fabulously snarky opponent. Be that opponent.

14

(Unfortunately) Trotsky's Advice Is Relevant Today

Trotsky had a front-row seat to the rise of authoritarianism in the 1920s and 1930s. Across Europe, fascism was on the march, and he saw firsthand how it crushed workers' movements, consolidated power, and silenced dissent.

 Trotsky's Advice

Look for the "solutions" being offered. Fascists always blame "the other"—immigrants, minorities, or political opponents—while promising a return to some mythical golden age.

 Your Move

If you hear this, challenge the narrative. Point out the real causes of the crisis (hint: it's usually the same people funding the fascist movement).

15

Historical Fascists You've Probably Heard of

Mussolini's Italy (1922): Benito Mussolini pioneered the fascist blueprint—crush unions, co-opt the middle class, and use violence to suppress any opposition. Trotsky observed how Mussolini manipulated a disillusioned population by blaming outsiders (Jews, communists, immigrants) for Italy's problems.

Hitler's Germany (1933): Adolf Hitler took Mussolini's playbook and gave it steroids. By the time the Nazis came to power, Trotsky was exiled from the Soviet Union and watching from afar. He warned repeatedly that Hitler's rise wasn't just a German problem but a global threat to workers and democracy everywhere.

Franco's Spain (1936): The Spanish Civil War became a battleground for fascists and anti-fascists. Trotsky saw Spain as a crucial moment for the left to stand united—but it was here that divisions within the socialist and communist movements (fueled in part by Stalin's meddling) proved disastrous.

16

How to Spot Fascist Regimes Today

Lessons to Remember

1
LESSON

The only way to stop fascism is through organized, united resistance. Divided opposition is doomed opposition.

2
LESSON

Authoritarian leaders manipulate economic despair and social divisions to seize power. Trotsky's call to unite workers, fight inequality, and confront fascism head-on remains as urgent as ever.

3
LESSON

Fascism is a tool of the ruling class. He warned that fascists aren't just "crazy people" or "extremists"; they're a reactionary force deployed by elites to crush revolution and maintain the status quo.

17

What Fascism looks like today: militarized mass movements, institutions hollowed out, mobs of everyday people whipped into a frenzy by elites who quietly bankroll their chaos.

Fascist movements are both grassroots and top-down. Think angry mobs of "everyday people" whipped into a frenzy by elites who quietly bankroll their chaos. Fascists don't outright destroy democratic institutions; they rot them from the inside. Judges, police chiefs, media outlets—they all start toeing the line. Paramilitary groups who use intimidation and violence to silence opposition. They're often dressed in matching outfits (or hats) and carry weapons.

18

Fighting Back Like a Girl Boss

Build Broad Coalitions

Building broad coalitions is essential when resisting fascism or authoritarianism because no single group can effectively combat such powerful, all-encompassing threats on its own. Here's why coalitions matter and how they strengthen resistance movements:

1. **Mobilize the Working Class**

   Trotsky believed the working class was the key to defeating fascism. Why? Because they're the ones fascists fear most. Educate, organize, and empower workers to resist. Fascism feeds on despair, so give people a reason to hope—and a path to action.

2. **Get involved**

   Join in grassroots organizing, unions, and community movements. This is where the real power lies.

3. **Be Ruthlessly Realistic**

19

Trotsky didn't believe in "waiting it out" or hoping fascists would just implode. He warned that complacency was fatal. Fight now, fight hard, and don't stop until the movement is dismantled. Fascists gain strength the longer they're allowed to exist.

Think of it like pest control. You don't just "let termites do their thing"—you call in the professionals and eradicate the problem.

Conclusion: Why Does Trotsky Still Matter?

Trotsky knew that fascism preys on fear and division. But he also knew that organized, determined people could bring it down. The good news? You're not powerless. History has shown that when we fight fascism together, we win.

So, take a deep breath, channel your inner Trotsky, and remember: the best way to stop fascism is to see it for what it is—and then take action.

WHAT YOU CAN DO ABOUT IT
Challenge their narrative

Don't let fascist regimes dictate the narrative. Challenge every half-truth, mischaracterization, and outright lie you encounter. Vigilance is our strongest defense against their gaslighting—only by calling out their distortions can we dismantle their control over the truth.

1. **It's Economic Inequality not Immigrants or the Woke**

   The Problem: Widening income gaps, stagnant wages, and a lack of upward mobility leave people feeling desperate and disenfranchised.

   ☐ *Learn the facts:* Share statistics about wealth inequality, CEO pay gaps, and the declining power of unions

   ☐ *Speak up locally:* Advocate for higher minimum wages, fair tax policies, and corporate accountability in your city and state.

   ☐ *Support labor movements:* Join, donate to, or amplify union efforts.

2. **It's Fear of Cultural Change not an Attack on Family Values**

   The Problem: Shifting demographics, greater visibility for marginalized groups, and changing social norms make some people feel like their identity or way of life is "under attack."

21

- [ ] *Reframe the narrative:* Emphasize how diversity and inclusion enrich communities and economies.

- [ ] *Confront lies:* Fact-check and challenge falsehoods about marginalized groups on social media or in conversation.

- [ ] *Support inclusive policies:* Advocate for equity in education, healthcare, and workplace protections for all.

3. **It's Corruption & Lack of Accountability not Weak Leadership**

The Problem: Government and corporate corruption erode public trust, leaving people cynical and disengaged.

- [ ] *Demand transparency:* Call and write to representatives to support anti-corruption laws and campaign finance reform.

- [ ] *Amplify watchdogs:* Share reports and insights from groups like the ACLU, ProPublica, and OpenSecrets.

- [ ] *Engage locally:* Attend city council meetings or school board discussions to hold local leaders accountable.

4. **Misinformation & Media Manipulation not Fake News**

22

The Problem: Fascists rely on disinformation to confuse and divide the public, using social media, partisan news outlets, and even bots to spread lies.

☐ *Educate yourself:* Learn how to spot fake news, verify sources, and avoid sharing unverified information.

☐ *Support independent journalism:* Subscribe to and promote reputable, nonpartisan news outlets.

☐ *Be a fact-checker:* Politely correct misinformation online and in conversations, using credible sources.

5. Polarization and Division not Us vs. Them

The Problem: Fascists thrive on an "us vs. them" mentality, turning neighbors into enemies.

☐ *Build bridges:* Engage in meaningful conversations with people across political divides, focusing on shared values and concerns.

☐ *Highlight common enemies:* Redirect anger toward corporate greed, systemic corruption, and erosion of rights.

☐ *Be a unifier:* Support organizations and leaders who promote bipartisanship and community-building.

23

6. Manufactured Crises not "We're Under Attack!"

The Problem: Fascists create or exaggerate crises—whether about immigration, crime, or national security—to justify authoritarian policies. Beware a sudden crisis or attack from inside or outside the US

☐ *Expose the false narratives:* Share data that debunks claims about crime rates, immigration, or other "crises."

☐ *Focus on real issues:* Redirect conversations toward systemic problems like healthcare, housing, or climate change.

☐ *Be vigilant:* Monitor proposed policies for hidden authoritarian agendas, like surveillance laws or limits on protests.

Turning Back the Clock, One Woman at a Time

If there's one thing authoritarian regimes love, it's control. And what's the fastest way to control a population? Start with the women. Strip their rights, dictate their roles, and you've already got a society primed for domination.

> When women have equality and autonomy, they don't stay quiet. Empowered women lead movements, demand accountability, and call out oppression for what it is.

It's not subtle, and it's definitely not new. From the Nazis demanding women pump out "pure" babies to modern leaders slashing reproductive rights and calling it "tradition," it's the same tired playbook, century after century.

Get Up, Rise Up, Don't give Up the Fight

History also tells another story—one the fascists would love to erase. When the world has tried to shove women into the shadows, they've stepped into the spotlight instead.

They've resisted, protested, and fought back, sometimes with rallies and petitions, sometimes with underground networks, and sometimes with sheer audacity.

This chapter is your crash course in what's really at stake and why women fighting back isn't just about holding the line—it's about shaping a future where we aren't just surviving, but thriving.

Because here's the truth: if fascists come for the women first, it's because they're terrified of what happens when women rise up.

So the first step in building an authoritarian state is knocking women back a few pegs—redefining them as second-class citizens whose worth is tied to their wombs, not their voices. It's not just about controlling women; it's about sending a warning: if we can do this to them, we can do it to anyone.

> *If fascists come for the women first, it's because they're terrified of what happens when women rise up.*

26

If fascists had a playbook, page one would say: "Control the women, control the future."

What a Girl's Gotta Know

Women are the backbone of society—raising kids, building communities, and pushing progress forward. That's why authoritarian regimes have always used patriarchy as a blunt-force tool to dismantle their power.

The Fascist Playbook: A Modern Attack on Women's Rights

If fascism is about control, then women's rights are the first casualty. Modern authoritarian regimes may dress their actions in the language of "tradition" or "morality," but the goal is the same: strip women of their autonomy, silence their voices, and shove them back into roles that make them easier to manage. Sound familiar? It should. They've been running this play forever.

If fascists had a playbook, page one would say: "Control the women, control the future."

■ **STEP ONE:
USE PATRIARCHY
AS A WEAPON**

Women are the backbone of society—raising kids, building communities, and pushing progress forward. That's why authoritarian regimes have always used patriarchy as a blunt-force tool to dismantle their power.

Take Nazi Germany, for example. Hitler's vision for women boiled down to three K's: *Kinder, Küche, Kirche* (Children, Kitchen, Church). Women were rewarded with medals for birthing more Aryan babies, like motherhood was some kind of dystopian Olympics. Want a career? An education? Tough luck. Your job was to create the next generation of obedient citizens.

The same tactics popped up in Mussolini's Italy and Franco's Spain. Women were shoved out of the workforce and told their patriotic duty was to "restore family values." In reality, this was code for "stay dependent, stay quiet, and don't challenge the system." The message was loud and clear: women belong in the home, not in the conversation.

29

■ **STEP TWO: CONTROL WOMEN'S BODIES**

Who gives birth, when, and how? That's power.

Authoritarian regimes love micromanaging women's bodies because it gives them control over society. Denying access to contraception or abortion isn't about "morality" or "tradition"— it's a calculated move to keep women in check.

Reproductive rights are usually the first target. Without control over their own bodies, women are trapped in cycles of poverty and dependence, making it harder for them to push back against the regime. Healthcare follows close behind. When access to maternal care, contraception, or even basic preventative screenings is gutted, women are left fighting for survival instead of fighting for justice.

■ **STEP THREE: KILL EDUCATION, KILL RESISTANCE**

The easiest way to silence a population? Don't let them learn how to ask questions.

That's why education for girls is often one of the first casualties under authoritarian regimes. By denying women the tools to think critically, they

30

ensure half the population can't challenge the system.

From closing schools for girls to spreading propaganda about women's "natural roles," the goal is always the same: make women smaller, quieter, and easier to control. An uneducated population is a compliant population, and that's exactly what authoritarian regimes want.

Bodily Autonomy Under Siege

■ **Step Four: Attack Reproductive Rights**

One of the easiest ways to control women is to control their bodies. Today's authoritarian regimes (and their wannabes) are masters of this. From banning abortion to restricting contraception, they're not just rolling back rights—they're rolling back decades of progress.

Case in point: the wave of abortion bans in the United States. States like Texas and Alabama have passed draconian laws that don't just outlaw abortion but punish anyone who helps—a doctor, a friend, even an Uber driver. It's not

31

about "protecting life." It's about controlling women and forcing them into roles they didn't choose.

Limit Access to Healthcare

Access to healthcare isn't just a right—it's survival. And yet, authoritarian regimes consistently underfund or outright deny women's access to maternal care, contraception, and even basic preventative screenings. It's no coincidence. Healthy women can fight back. Sick women can't.

Take Poland, where extreme restrictions on abortion were legislated by their fascist leader, Jarosław Kaczyński. Restrictions that have led to a maternal health crisis. Women denied life-saving care because doctors fear prosecution is the grim reality of authoritarian overreach. It's not just barbaric—it's calculated.

32

Economic inequality is used as a tool.

■ **STEP SIX:**
ECONOMIC
INEQUALITY

The wage gap isn't just a sad statistic—it's a weapon. Authoritarian regimes love economic inequality because it keeps women financially dependent and, by extension, easier to control. Wage disparities, lack of access to high-paying jobs, and rampant discrimination aren't bugs in the system—they're features.

Even in supposedly progressive democracies, women earn less for the same work. Now imagine what happens when authoritarian leaders amplify this inequality. They restrict education and job opportunities, making it nearly impossible for women to achieve financial independence.

33

The Wage Gap Is Not an Accident

Why Target Women?

Women represent autonomy, progress, and social change—all things authoritarian regimes hate. Controlling women isn't just about them; it's about sending a message to everyone else. If they can take away women's rights, they can do it to anyone.

But here's what they don't count on: women fighting back. From underground education networks to mass protests for reproductive rights, women have always resisted. And when they do, they don't just disrupt the regime—they expose its deepest fear: a future it can't control.

Undermining judicial independence, stoking nationalism, and targeting marginalized groups like women are hallmarks of modern right-wing populism and illiberal democracy.

2016 Poland Bans All Abortions: In 2016, the Law and Justice Party (PiS) supported legislation aimed at banning abortion under all circumstances, including cases of fetal defects. This proposal faced significant public backlash, leading to widespread protests known as the "Black Protests." The intense opposition resulted in the withdrawal of the proposed legislation and the eventual loss of power of the PiS.

36

Unpaid Labor:
The Invisible Anchor

Here's the kicker: even when women **are** working, they're still expected to do the majority of unpaid domestic labor. Cooking, cleaning, caregiving–it's all on them. This double burden isn't just exhausting; it's a strategy to keep women too overworked to resist.

During the COVID-19 pandemic, millions of women left the workforce because they couldn't juggle it all. Authoritarian leaders noticed. The more women are tied to the home, the less they're out organizing, protesting, or running for office.

Building Broad Coalitions

"A FEARLESS INDOMITABLE RACE."
WILLIAM ROONEY.

Whether it's on the streets, in courtrooms, or online, women are fighting back. And every time they do, they chip away at the structures designed to oppress them. Because the one thing authoritarian regimes fear more than empowered women? Empowered women who refuse to quit.

STORYTIME

Women, Life, Freedom Movement

Imagine being told what to wear, how to behave, and how much of yourself you're allowed to show—and if you resist, you risk prison, torture, or worse. That's the reality Iranian women have faced under strict laws mandating hijabs and policing their behavior. But in September 2022, when 22-year-old Mahsa Amini died in custody after being arrested by the morality police, Iranian women said, "Enough."

The streets erupted in protests led by women—young and old, hijab-wearing and not—chanting "Women, Life, Freedom." Their defiance wasn't just about headscarves; it was about demanding the right to exist as equals, to control their own lives, and to live without fear. Women burned their hijabs in bonfires, cut their hair in public, and stared down security forces armed with guns and tear gas.

Despite brutal crackdowns—including arrests, beatings, and killings—these women keep showing up. They're not just protesting for them-

39

selves but for a future where their daughters won't have to live in fear. Their courage has ignited a global movement, reminding the world that when women fight for freedom, they do it with fire in their hearts—and sometimes literal fire in the streets.

Silencing Women's Voices

Protest? Prepare for a Crackdown

When women organize, they disrupt the status quo. And authoritarian regimes hate that. Across the globe, we've seen crackdowns on women's protests, whether it's for reproductive rights, gender equality, or freedom of speech.

Take Iran's "Women, Life, Freedom" movement. Women have risked imprisonment, torture, and death to protest against mandatory hijab laws and systemic oppression. The regime's response? Brutal crackdowns, including violence and mass arrests. But these women aren't backing down—and their bravery is inspiring a global movement.

Journalists, Activists, and Politicians as Targets

Women who speak out often pay the highest price. Female journalists, activists, and politicians are disproportionately targeted for violence, harassment, and imprisonment. Why? Because authoritarian regimes know that silencing these voices silences entire movements.

Look at Maria Ressa, the Filipino journalist who exposed Duterte's authoritarian tactics through her reporting. She faced harassment, legal charges, and threats, but she kept going—and won a Nobel Peace Prize for her efforts. Women like her remind us that speaking truth to power is dangerous, but also essential.

STORYTIME

FIGHTING FOR THE TRUTH

Maria Ressa

had two choices: stay silent and stay safe, or speak out and risk everything. As the co-founder of *Rappler*, a news outlet in the Philippines, she chose the second option—and it's made her one of the most relentless voices against authoritarianism.

During Rodrigo Duterte's presidency, Ressa and her team exposed his government's bloody war on drugs, where thousands were killed without trial. They uncovered how the regime manipulated social media to spread propaganda and silence dissent.

The price of her truth-telling? Arrests, harassment, and a barrage of lawsuits aimed at bankrupting her and her organization. But Maria Ressa didn't back down. She kept reporting, kept speaking out, and kept telling the world what was happening in her country.

In 2021, her efforts earned her the Nobel Peace Prize, making her the first Filipino journalist to receive it. Her message is clear: freedom of the press isn't just a journalist's fight—it's everyone's fight.

Because when the truth is silenced, authoritarianism wins.

Maria reminds us that bravery isn't about being fearless—it's about speaking out, even when the odds are stacked against you. In her words:

"We have to fight for the truth, because the truth is what holds power to account." And fight she does.

42

Profiles in Resistance

Throughout history, when authoritarian regimes have tried to silence dissent, women have stepped in and turned the volume all the way up. They've protested, organized, and fought back—sometimes with the world watching, sometimes in secret. This section highlights three groups of women who didn't just survive oppression—they defied it, inspiring countless others to resist.

Narges Mohammadi
A Voice They Can't Silence

Let's talk about Narges Mohammadi, the human rights activist who refuses to stay quiet—literally. Despite facing imprisonment, solitary confinement, and torture in Iran, Narges keeps raising her voice for justice. Her fight is focused on the abolition of the death penalty and the rights of women and political prisoners in a country where speaking out can cost you everything.

43

Narges has been arrested so many times that you'd think the regime would have figured out by now: locking her up doesn't stop her. From behind bars, she's written letters, spoken out about the conditions of female prisoners, and called for reform. Her courage earned her the 2023 Nobel Peace Prize, but let's be clear—Narges isn't doing this for awards. She's fighting for a future where women aren't afraid to live freely.

Her resilience is a reminder that even when the world tries to shut you down, your voice can be the loudest act of defiance.

At just 15 years old, Malala Yousafzai was shot in the head for one simple reason: she wanted to go to school. The Taliban thought that would be the end of her story. Instead, it was just the beginning.

Malala Yousafzai
The Girl Who Survived & Thrived

44

Malala didn't just survive the assassination attempt; she turned her pain into purpose. Today, she's a global advocate for girls' education, a Nobel Peace Prize laureate, and a living, breathing middle finger to every dictator who's ever tried

to keep women uneducated and powerless.

Her activism is rooted in a simple but radical idea: every girl deserves an education. Through the Malala Fund, she's helping girls in marginalized communities access schools, books, and teachers—things authoritarian regimes often deny to women. Malala's fight isn't just

45

about education; it's about empowerment. Because when you educate a girl, you're arming her with the tools to challenge the system—and that's what terrifies authoritarian regimes the most.

What do you do when your government kidnaps your children and denies they ever existed? If you're the Mothers of the Plaza de Mayo, you show up every single week, wearing white headscarves and holding pictures of your missing loved ones, demanding answers.

Mothers of the Plaza de Mayo

Grief Turned into Resistance

During Argentina's brutal dictatorship in the 1970s and 80s, tens of thousands of people—many of them young activists—were "disappeared" by the regime. While the country lived in fear, these women turned their grief into resistance. Every Thursday, they marched in

46

Resistance isn't one size fits all

Buenos Aires' Plaza de Mayo, directly in front of the presidential palace, refusing to let the world forget what was happening.

The regime tried to dismiss them as "crazy old ladies," but their persistence worked. They brought international attention to the atrocities and inspired other movements worldwide to use maternal activism as a form of protest. The Mothers of the Plaza de Mayo proved that love and grief are powerful motivators—and that even in the face of terror, women will fight for justice.

The Bigger Picture

Healthcare, economic inequality, and silencing women's voices aren't random acts—they're pieces of a larger strategy to dismantle women's power. When women lose autonomy, when they're overworked and underpaid, when their voices are silenced, they're easier to control. But here's the thing: history shows that women don't stay silent for long.

What does resistance look like?

Sometimes it's a Nobel laureate speaking to the United Nations. Sometimes it's a mother marching with a photograph. Sometimes it's a woman writing letters from a prison cell.

Because when women resist, they don't just change their circumstances—they inspire the world to do better.

49

What's at Stake

Let's be real: fascists are like toddlers with a box of crayons. They're messy, destructive, and obsessed with drawing lines between people. The more divided we are, the easier it is for them to swoop in and take control.

When women's rights are attacked, it's not just about controlling women—it's about controlling everyone.

When women's rights are attacked, it's not just about controlling women—it's about controlling *everyone*. Stripping women of their autonomy is like pulling the first thread in the fabric of democracy. The unraveling doesn't stop there. And guess who feels the brunt of it first? Marginalized groups. If you think this fight is only about women, think again.

50

Loss of Autonomy = Loss of Democracy

Here's the deal: women's equality isn't just a nice-to-have—it's a cornerstone of a healthy democracy. Why? Because when women are empowered, entire communities thrive. They run for office, organize protests, and advocate for change. Women's voices aren't just part of the conversation—they shape it.

Authoritarian regimes know this, which is why they go after women first. It's not a coincidence that stripping reproductive rights, restricting healthcare, and blocking women's access to education often come alongside attacks on voting rights, press freedom, and other democratic pillars. It's all connected.

Look at history. When women lose their autonomy, society doesn't just take a step back—it tumbles down a slippery slope. Nazi Germany started with policies controlling women's repro-ductive roles, and it wasn't long before they were silencing entire groups. Modern authoritarian regimes follow the same playbook: control women, weaken democracy, and consolidate power.

When women's rights are eroded, it's a warning shot. If half the population can't make decisions about their own bodies, how long before the rest of society loses the ability to make decisions about anything?

51

Divide & Conquer: The Fascist's Favorite Trick. Fascists win when we fight each other. It's that simple. They love stoking division.

Men vs. women, cis vs. trans, Black vs. white, rich vs. poor—because while we're busy pointing fingers, they're consolidating power. They don't care about tradition or morality; they care about control. And what better way to control people than to keep them too busy fighting to notice what's really happening?

When women's rights are under attack, it's not just about women. It's about setting a precedent. If they can take away autonomy from one group, they'll come for the next. Today it's abortion bans; tomorrow it's LGBTQ+ rights, voting rights, or basic privacy. Fascism doesn't stop—it snowballs.

52

Privilege Won't Save You (Unless You're a Billionaire)

Think your privilege is a get-out-of-jail-free card? Not under fascism. Sure, the billionaires are safe–they're the ones writing the rules. But for the rest of us, privilege gets redistributed in the worst way possible: straight into the hands of the elite.

White, middle-class, heterosexual folks, take note: you're not exempt. Fascist regimes don't play favorites; they play survival of the richest.

That "good job" you worked hard for? Gone, because now it's about loyalty to the state, not merit.

Your "safe community"? Say hello to surveillance and militarization. Fascism strips privilege from everyone but the ultra-rich and ultra-powerful.

The Glue That Holds Us Together

So, how do we fight back? Unity. And not the kumbaya, hold-hands-and-sing kind. Real, gritty, intersectional unity. Fascists are terrified of us coming together because they know it's the only thing strong enough to stop them.

When we recognize that women's rights are connected to LGBTQ+ rights, racial justice, and economic equality, we stop seeing our struggles as separate battles. Instead, we form a movement—a loud, unstoppable force that doesn't fall for the divide-and-conquer playbook.

Look at every successful resistance movement: from the Mothers of the Plaza de Mayo in Argentina to the protests in Iran, unity is what makes them powerful. The more we support each other, the harder we are to silence.

We're Stronger Together

Fascists want us silent, divided, and powerless—but they've underestimated us. Women have always led the fight for justice, toppling regimes and rewriting history. This isn't just about defending our rights; it's about building a future where equality and freedom aren't up for debate.

The fascists may have their playbooks, but guess what? So do we. And ours is filled with strategies that are smart, creative, and most importantly, effective. Resisting authoritarianism isn't just about outrage—it's about action. Here's how to turn your frustration into fuel and fight back like the unstoppable force you are.

First Rule of Resistance Club: Don't Go It Alone

Building a community—whether it's in your neighborhood, online, or globally—is the backbone of any successful movement. Fascists thrive on isolation and fear, so the best way to counter them is to connect with others.

Start small. Join or create local groups focused on women's rights, LGBTQ+ advocacy, or racial justice. Go to town halls, protest planning meetings, or even just book clubs where people care about the issues. Use social media to amplify your reach, but don't stop there—real change happens when people show up in person.

Every movement starts with people coming together, sharing stories, and saying, "We're not going to take this." Be one of those people.

What Works:

- Organizing protests and rallies.
- Supporting mutual aid networks to help vulnerable communities.
- Connecting with global organizations to share resources and strategies.

56

Humor as a Weapon: Laugh Them Into Oblivion

Fascists hate being laughed at. Why? Because their power depends on fear, and nothing deflates fear like a good belly laugh. Satire and dark humor have always been tools of resistance, from underground anti-Nazi cartoons to modern memes mocking authoritarian leaders.

Just remember, humor is like spice—use it wisely. Punch up, not down. Target the oppressors, not the oppressed.

When you make fun of fascists, you expose the absurdity of their policies. You take away the illusion of invincibility they try so hard to maintain. And let's be honest: authoritarianism is inherently ridiculous. Their obsession with controlling every aspect of people's lives is practically begging for parody.

What Works

- Create and share memes that mock oppressive policies.

- Use satire to highlight the hypocrisy of authoritarian leaders.

- Join or follow comedy platforms that use humor to resist (think John Oliver or political TikTok).

Education & Advocacy: Arm Yourself with Knowledge

The Best Weapon Against Fascism is An Informed Citizenry.

Fascists love ignorance—it makes their propaganda easier to sell. The more people understand what's really going on, the harder it is for authoritarian regimes to tighten their grip. That's why education and advocacy are non-negotiable in any resistance movement.

Start by educating yourself and those around you. Know your rights, the policies that threaten them, and the history of resistance movements. Use that knowledge to call out misinformation and hold people accountable.

Knowledge is power, and in this fight, power is everything.

What Works:

- Host workshops on issues like reproductive rights, voter suppression, or media literacy.
- Share resources—books, articles, podcasts—that unpack the threats to democracy.
- Advocate for policies that protect women's rights by writing letters, signing petitions, or showing up to hearings.

58

Stay Awake: How Voting Shapes Policy and Drives Change

Here's the thing about dictators: They love it when you don't vote.

Authoritarians bank on low turnout and apathy to sneak their policies through. They gerrymander districts, suppress votes, and pass laws while everyone's distracted. Don't let them. Voting is one of the most powerful tools in your resistance arsenal, but it's only the start.

Beyond voting, you need to influence policy. Call your representatives. Demand accountability. Show up at city council meetings. Grassroots activism–things like canvassing, phone banking, and organizing local coalitions– turns individual votes into collective power.

Voting isn't glamorous, but it's how you protect rights, dismantle oppressive policies, and send a message to fascists: you don't get to run the show.

What Works:
- **Register voters, especially in marginalized communities.**
- **Push for policy changes that protect women's healthcare, education, and economic rights.**
- **Get involved in local politics–it's where the big changes start.**

59

Why Being Involved in Local Politics Matter the Most

Local Politics is Your Secret Weapon Against a Fascist Leader

Okay, so there's a wannabe dictator running the show at the national level. It's scary, frustrating, and makes you want to scream into a pillow. But here's the thing: local politics is where the magic happens. Yes, it's not as glamorous as protesting on the steps of the Capitol, but it's where you can actually make a difference—and fast. Here's why: consolidated power, and silenced dissent.

1. **Your Town, Your Rules (Sort Of):**
   Local governments control the stuff you deal with every day—schools, parks, roads, policing, public health. Fascist leaders might rant on TV, but your city council decides if your kids' textbooks are banned or your potholes are fixed.

2. **Local Leaders Can Say "Nope!"**
   A good mayor or city council can push back on oppressive national policies. Think sanctuary cities that protect immigrants or local resolutions that flip the bird to regressive laws.

3. **Movements Start Small:**
   Every big change you've ever heard of? It probably started in someone's garage or at a local meeting. When you organize

60

locally, you're planting the seeds for something way bigger.

RESISTANCE
IS IN OUR
DNA

4. Protect the Vulnerable:
When national leaders target specific groups, your community can step in. Local programs can offer resources, shelter, and support to those who need it most. You're literally saving lives here.

5. Resist, Girl, Resist:
A fascist leader wants everyone to roll over and give up. A strong, active community sends a loud message: Not today, Satan.

6. Real Change Starts Close to Home:
Winning local elections builds momentum. Want better state and national leaders? Help grow them locally first. You're like the political talent scout your town didn't know it needed.

7. Keep Democracy Alive:
National politics may feel like it's spiraling, but you can keep democracy alive in your backyard. Show up to town halls, vote in every local election, and remind your neighbors that apathy is how fascism wins.

61

They're watching. Authoritarians hate when communities take charge. Local resistance makes it harder for their big, bad policies to stick.

They want power centralized, so keep it messy, decentralized, and people-powered. Fascists want us silent, divided, and powerless—but they've underestimated us. Women have always led the fight for justice, toppling regimes and rewriting history. This isn't just about defending our rights; it's about building a future where equality and freedom aren't up for debate.

Stay informed. Stay connected. Stay unyielding. The clock isn't turning back—because we're too busy forging ahead. Together, we're unstoppable. Let's keep fighting, keep rising, and show them what real power looks like.

62

Bottom lineGetting involved in local politics isn't just important—it's badass. You're protecting your community, amplifying your voice, and proving that even in the face of chaos, you've got the power to fight back. Start small, think big, and don't let anyone tell you your city council meeting isn't worth your time. Because it is.

Resistance is a team sport

Resisting fascism isn't about doing everything—it's about doing **something**. Organize your community, laugh at their absurdity, educate yourself and others, and make your voice heard at the polls. Every act of resistance, no matter how small, chips away at authoritarian control.

Together, we're not just fighting back—we're building a world they can't take away. And the best part? They know it. So let's get to work.

63

The Informed Girl's Playbook: Stay Ahead of Propaganda

In a world where a fascist regime controls the flow of information like a DJ spinning their own propaganda playlist, staying informed becomes a battle for truth. News is no longer just skewed—it's weaponized, with disinformation and censorship designed to confuse, manipulate, and silence dissent.

But you don't have to let their fake news machine dominate your mind—or your democracy. Here's your guide to breaking through the noise, spotting propaganda traps, and safeguarding your access to real, reliable information.

Next Up: Spotting Propaganda Like a Pro →

The Gaslighting Olympics

Propaganda isn't just about flashy posters or over-the-top speeches anymore—it's TikToks, memes, and viral hashtags. It's trolls who start arguments in the chats and bots who get accounts taken down. Fascists have adapted to the digital age, but with the right tools, you can spot their tricks faster than you can say, "That's a red flag."

65

Red Flags of Propaganda

1. Emotional Manipulation

Content designed to make you angry, scared, or super patriotic (cue the swelling violins) is likely trying to bypass your logic.

How to Spot It: Ask yourself, "Is this trying to inform me or manipulate me?"

2. Over-simplification

"They're the problem, and here's a one-word solution!" Propaganda thrives on turning complex issues into black-and-white narratives.

How to Spot It: Look for missing context, unsupported claims, or buzzwords like "invasion" or "crisis."

3. Echo Chamber

If everyone in your feed agrees and it feels a little too good, you're probably in an echo chamber. Propaganda loves those.

How to Spot It: Follow diverse voices, even ones you disagree with, to keep your perspective balanced.

Your Move

- **Fact-check, Always:** Bookmark sites like Snopes, PolitiFact, and FactCheck.org to sniff out bogus claims.

- **Slow Down Before Sharing:** Misinformation spreads when we react instead of reflect. Take 30 seconds to verify before you post. If you do post something that turns out to be propaganda, delete it if you can. If you can't, post a correction. Acknowledge the mistake so future readers don't fall for it based on your recommendation!

- **Be a Mythbuster:** Gently correct misinformation in your circles—especially in group chats where bad takes breed like rabbits.

67

Reliable Sources in a Fake-News World

In a sea of "alternative facts," you need a lifeboat. Here's where to go for trustworthy info that won't steer you into a propaganda iceberg.

The Gold Standard

- **Associated Press (AP):** Just the facts, ma'am. AP delivers straightforward news without the spin.
- **Reuters:** Like AP, but with an international flair.
- **BBC:** A global perspective that's less likely to be biased by U.S. politics.

Investigative Powerhouses

- **ProPublica:** Deep dives into corruption, corporate greed, and government misdeeds.
- **NPR:** Balanced, well-researched reporting with a softer tone.

Independent Voices

- **Democracy Now!:** Progressive and grassroots-focused reporting.
- **The Intercept:** Investigative journalism that pulls no punches.
- **Drop Site News:** An independent news outlet focusing on war and politics in the U.S. and globally.

68

- **Zeteo:** Founded by journalist Mehdi Hasan in early 2024, Zeteo is a media company delivering independent and unfiltered news.

- **The Cradle:** A news website dedicated to covering the Middle East, providing in-depth analysis and reporting on regional politics, conflicts, and socio-economic developments. It aims to offer perspectives often underrepresented in mainstream media.

- **Rest of the World:** A nonprofit journalism organization that reports on the impact of technology beyond the Western world.

- **Ground News:** A news aggregation platform that provides readers with diverse perspectives on current events. It aggregates news stories from various sources, highlighting differences in coverage and potential biases, enabling users to gain a more comprehensive understanding of the news landscape.

- **Grist:** An independent, nonprofit media organization dedicated to reporting on climate solutions and environmental justice.

- **The Lever:** An American reader-supported investigative news outlet. Its mission is to hold power accountable by reporting on how corporate influence affects society.

- **Substack:** There are many, many independant journalists writing on Substack that are worth investigating.

69

But Are These Still Trusted Sources?

The Washington Post, The New York Times, and *The Atlantic* are still generally considered trusted outlets, but it's important to approach their reporting with an informed and critical perspective. As with any source, it's important to engage critically, recognize potential biases, and supplement with diverse perspectives to get a well-rounded understanding. Here's what to keep in mind:

Corporate Ownership

The Washington Post is owned by Jeff Bezos, raising questions about potential conflicts of interest when it comes to coverage of Amazon or broader corporate power. During the 2024 presidential election, Bezos prohibited the Washington Post from endorsing the Democratic candidate. The only other time the paper did not endorse a presidential candidate in the past 44 years was in 1988.

The New York Times is primarily owned by the Ochs-Sulzberger family, who have maintained control since Adolph Ochs acquired the newspaper in 1896. However, some critics argue that such concentrated ownership might lead to biases aligning with the family's perspectives, and that because it is publicly traded on the stock market, that can influence reporting.

70

The Atlantic is owned by Laurene Powell Jobs. She acquired a majority stake in the publication through her organization, Emerson Collective. Emerson Collective focuses on a range of social issues, including education, immigration reform, environmental conservation, and media, using a combination of philanthropy, impact investing, and advocacy to drive meaningful change.

Editorial Bias:

While they strive for objectivity, their editorial boards have clear slants:

> **The Washington Post:** Generally leans centrist to left, with a strong focus on democracy and accountability.

> **The New York Times:** Also leans left, particularly on social and cultural issues, though recently its biases have been showing. Try to find another source for alternative perspectives.

> **The Atlantic:** Offers a mix of centrist, left-leaning, and libertarian perspectives, but with a clear bias toward Western liberal democracy.

Potential for Framing Bias

> Like all media, these outlets frame stories based on their target audience's values and interests. Be aware of how narratives may emphasize certain angles while down-playing others.

71

How to Use Them Wisely

Read Critically

Pay attention to how stories are framed and consider
what might be left out. Compare coverage of the same
story across multiple outlets.

Pair with Other Sources:

Balance these outlets with other trusted sources like AP,
Reuters, or BBC to get a broader perspective.

Focus on Investigative Pieces:

Their in-depth investigative reporting is often their
strongest work and less influenced by the quick-turn-
around demands of daily news cycles.

Mix It Up: Avoid the Echo Chamber

No single source has a monopoly on truth. Even the best outlets have biases shaped by their editorial boards, funding sources, or geographical perspectives. Relying on a single source can lead to blind spots or skewed views.

Blend Mainstream and Independent Sources:

Pair trusted mainstream outlets (like AP, Reuters, and BBC) with investigative or niche outlets (such as ProPublica, Democracy Now!, or newspapers or Substack columnists).

Go International:

U.S.-based media often centers domestic concerns. Add international outlets like Al Jazeera, The Guardian, or Deutsche Welle to your reading list for a broader context and perspective.

Read Across the Political Spectrum:

Even if you disagree with a source's political slant, checking outlets from both sides can reveal differences in framing and help you identify bias.

73

Why
It Matters

By diversifying your sources, you avoid
echo chambers and propaganda traps.
The more angles you understand, the
harder it is for disinformation to take root.

Support Quality Journalism. A free and independent press is democracy's watchdog. Supporting quality journalism ensures that vital stories get told—even when they challenge powerful interests.

High-quality journalism is expensive to produce. Investigative reporting, foreign correspondents, and thorough fact-checking require resources. If we don't support ethical journalism, we risk losing it to clickbait, misinformation, and partisan hacks.

75

How to Support the Press

Subscribe to Trusted Publications: Paying for outlets like The Washington Post, The New York Times, or The Atlantic ensures they can continue producing in-depth reporting.

Donate to Nonprofits: Nonprofit organizations like ProPublica, Mother Jones, or your local NPR station rely on public contributions to fund their work.

Don't Forget Local News: Local newspapers often break the stories that matter most to your community. Subscribe, share, and amplify their work.

Subscribe to independant journalists: Some of our best journalists now write their own blogs or publications, which can be found on platforms like Substack. Subscribing to these journalists means the editors and owners of giant media conglomerates can't suppress their views.

Think Critically About the News

Even the most reputable sources can make mistakes or inadvertently frame stories with bias. Being a critical consumer means engaging with the news thoughtfully and questioning narratives. And once the fascist leadership has got it's fingers into it, even the most reputable publications will not be trustworthy. (See Corporate Ownership and Jeff Bezo's interference with The Washington Post, above.)

Tips for Staying Critical

- **Read Beyond the Headline:** Headlines are designed to grab attention but often oversimplify. Always dive into the full story for context.

- **Verify Sources:** Ask, "Who wrote this? Are credible sources cited? What's the agenda behind this piece?"

- **Fact-Check Breaking News:** Early reports during unfolding events can be incomplete or inaccurate. Wait for verified updates before forming opinions.

77

- **Identify Patterns of Bias:** If a source consistently downplays or exaggerates certain topics, take note and adjust how you interpret their reporting.

Why It Matters

Engaging critically with the news doesn't mean rejecting it–it means understanding it fully. This is especially crucial when disinformation and propaganda aim to manipulate public opinion.

Staying informed in today's world takes effort, but it's worth it. By diversifying your sources, supporting ethical journalism, and thinking critically, you'll be better equipped to resist propaganda and fight back against disinformation.

78

Section 1: Privacy

In a world where surveillance has become a sport for authoritarian regimes, protecting your privacy isn't just for hackers and spies—it's essential for everyone. Whether you're organizing protests, quietly resisting in your daily life, or simply trying to keep your head down and survive, failing to secure your personal information can make you a target. Fascist governments thrive on control, and the tools of modern surveillance—facial recognition, social media tracking, and digital snooping—give them unprecedented power to identify, intimidate, and silence dissent.

Protecting your privacy isn't just about staying safe; it's about preserving your freedom to think, speak, and act without fear of retaliation. In a world where a single misstep can put you on the radar, it's critical to understand how to guard your digital and physical footprint. Fascists rely on fear, but with the right tools and practices, you can deny them the power to wield it.

STORYTIME

Hong Kong 2019-2020 Protests Against Extradition Law

Agnes Chow Ting

born in 1996, became one of the most recognizable figures in Hong Kong's pro-democracy movement, often referred to as the "Goddess of Democracy" by her supporters. A co-founder of the now-disband-

80

ed Demosistō party, Chow has been a prominent voice advocating for democratic reforms and opposing Beijing's increasing control over Hong Kong.

Early Activism: From Scholarism to Demosistō

Chow's activism began in her teenage years as a member of **Scholarism**, a student activist group led by Joshua Wong. In 2012, she was part of the movement opposing Beijing's attempt to impose "patriotic education" in Hong Kong schools. This marked her first step into the spotlight as a vocal critic of Beijing's policies.

In 2016, Chow co-founded **Demosistō** alongside Wong and Nathan Law. The party called for self-determination for Hong Kong and sought to empower young people to fight for their political future. Chow, with her eloquence and calm demeanor, quickly became a symbol of hope for many young Hongkongers.

The 2019 Protests and Arrests

When the 2019 anti-extradition bill protests erupted, Chow and Demosistō played key roles in mobilizing citizens. The proposed bill, which would have allowed extradition of Hong Kong residents to mainland China, sparked widespread fear about the erosion of the city's judicial independence.

Chow's involvement in the protests made her a prime target for Beijing. She was arrested multiple times, including in **August 2019**, when she was charged with "inciting others to participate in an unau-

81

thorized assembly" during a demonstration outside a police station. Despite facing legal consequences, Chow continued to advocate for peaceful resistance and international awareness of Hong Kong's plight.

National Security Law and Imprisonment

The passage of Beijing's **National Security Law in 2020** marked a turning point in Hong Kong's autonomy. The law criminalized acts of "secession, subversion, terrorism, and collusion with foreign forces," effectively silencing dissent. Demosistō disbanded shortly after its enactment, as its leaders feared prosecution under the sweeping law.

Chow was arrested under the National Security Law in **August 2020**, accused of colluding with foreign forces. Her arrest drew international condemnation, with human rights organizations denouncing it as an attack on free speech and peaceful activism.

In **December 2020**, Chow was sentenced to **10 months in prison** for her role in protests outside Hong Kong police headquarters. Her imprisonment highlighted the risks faced by pro-democracy activists under Beijing's crackdown.

Impact and Legacy

Agnes Chow's resilience and dedication to democracy have inspired countless people in Hong Kong and beyond. Even after her release from prison in **June 2021**, she remains under heavy surveillance and has largely avoided public appearances due to fear of re-arrest. However, her story continues to resonate as a testament to the courage and determination of those who stand against authoritarianism.

Why Her Story Matters

Agnes Chow's journey underscores the immense personal cost of standing up to a powerful regime. Her willingness to sacrifice her freedom for the future of her city exemplifies the power of youth-led movements and the enduring fight for democracy. Her story reminds us that the fight for freedom is ongoing—and that the world must not turn a blind eye to those on the front lines.

The Hong Kong protests showed that even small lapses in privacy—forgetting to turn off geolocation, using unsecured messaging apps, or posting on public social media—can have devastating consequences.

Activists and protesters worldwide must take proactive measures to protect their identities and communications to avoid similar fates.

"Arguing that you don't care about the right to privacy because you have nothing to hide is no different than saying you don't care about free speech because you have nothing to say."
-Edward Snowden

What a Girl's Gotta Know

Surveillance and the loss of privacy are tools for maintaining fascist or authoritarian regimes

Key Privacy Lessons for Modern Protesters

1. **Secure Your Communications:** Use encrypted messaging apps like Signal and ProtonMail to protect your identity.

2. **Avoid Traceable Devices:** Leave your phone at home or use a burner phone during protests to avoid geolocation tracking.

3. **Obscure Your Identity:** Wear masks, sunglasses, and hats to protect yourself from facial recognition.

4. **Compartmentalize Information:** Only share what others **need** to know to minimize risks if someone is compromised.

5. **Be Mindful of Digital Trails:** Avoid posting identifiable photos or information about protests on public platforms.

Apps & Tools to Stay Private

Fascists thrive on surveillance—it's their way to control narratives, track dissent, and enforce their agenda. But you don't have to play their game. With the right tools, you can protect your data, communicate securely, and explore the web without fear of being monitored. Stay informed, stay secure, and keep scrolling those memes with confidence.

For Private Browsing

DuckDuckGo

A search engine that respects your privacy by not tracking your searches or serving targeted ads. It also shows the same results to everyone, keeping search bias out of the equation. Pair it with its mobile app or browser extension for added privacy.

Brave Browser

This browser is built for privacy, blocking trackers, ads, and cookies by default. It also supports Tor for anonymous browsing directly in the app, making it a great all-in-one tool.

Firefox Focus

A minimalist browser that deletes your history, cookies, and trackers automatically after every session. It's a great option for quick, private browsing on the go.

For Secure Communication

Signal

This gold-standard messaging app offers end-to-end encryption for text, voice, and video chats. It's open-source and doesn't store metadata, so even if someone tried, they couldn't access your communication.

ProtonMail

A secure email service based in Switzerland, where privacy laws are strict. With end-to-end encryption and no data logging, ProtonMail is perfect for sensitive communication. Pair it with **ProtonVPN** for extra security.

For Staying Safe on Social Media

Jumbo

This privacy assistant app helps you clean up old social media posts, manage your privacy settings, and minimize your digital footprint. It's a great way to reduce what potential surveillance can uncover about you.

Tor Browser

If you want true anonymity online, the Tor Browser is your best bet. It routes your traffic through multiple servers, masking your IP address. Use it wisely—this tool is powerful but not foolproof if combined with careless browsing habits.

Tails OS

For the ultra-cautious, Tails is a portable operating system you can run from a USB stick. It leaves no trace of your activities and forces all internet connections through Tor.

For Fact-Checking

NewsGuard

This browser extension rates the credibility of websites and provides context about their ownership, funding, and journalistic practices. It's a great way to avoid falling for misinformation.

Ground News

Ground News offers a unique perspective by showing how different media outlets cover the same story. It highlights political bias and blind spots in reporting, helping you form a more nuanced understanding.

FactCheck.org & Snopes

Bookmark these trusted sites for debunking rumors, hoaxes, and fake news. They're invaluable for cutting through the noise of disinformation.

Additional Tools for Digital Privacy

VPNs (Virtual Private Networks)

A VPN encrypts your internet traffic and hides your IP address, making it harder for anyone to track your online activities. Some trustworthy options include **ExpressVPN, NordVPN,** and **ProtonVPN.**

Privacy Badger

A browser extension from the Electronic Frontier Foundation (EFF) that automatically blocks trackers and protects your browsing from surveillance.

Bitwarden

A password manager that ensures you use strong, unique passwords for every account. Weak passwords are one of the easiest ways for hackers to gain access to your data.

KeePassXC

For those who prefer an offline option, this open-source password manager keeps your credentials stored locally and safe from prying eyes.

91

Pro Tips for Staying Anonymous

Use Burner Accounts

Create separate email addresses and accounts for different purposes, especially for activism or dissent. Avoid linking these accounts to your real identity.

Disable Location Services

Many apps and devices track your location by default. Turn off location sharing whenever possible to protect your privacy.

Limit What You Share

Be mindful of what you post online. Even seemingly innocuous information can be pieced together to identify you.

Educate Yourself

Create separate email addresses and accounts for different purposes, especially for activism or dissent. Avoid linking these accounts to your real identity.

Practice Digital Hygiene

Many apps and devices track your location by default. Turn off location sharing whenever possible to protect your privacy.

Checklist for Staying Fabulously Private

☐ **Secure Your Browsing**

- Install and use a secure browser on every device (e.g. **Duck-DuckGo, Brave Browser, Tor Browser, Tails OS** or **Firefox Focus**)
- Don't forget to use one of these on your phone, too.

☐ **Encrypt Your Communication**

- Use **Signal** for secure messaging and calls.
- Switch to **ProtonMail** or **Session** for private, encrypted email.
- Install a VPN like **ExpressVPN** or **ProtonVPN** to encrypt all internet traffic.

☐ **Protect Social Media Privacy**

- Install **Jumbo** to clean up old posts and manage privacy settings.
- Avoid oversharing personal details online.
- Create burner accounts for activism or sensitive activities.

☐ **Fact-Check Information**

- Add NewsGuard to your browser for evaluating website credibility.
- Use **Ground News** to identify bias in news coverage.
- Bookmark **Snopes** and FactCheck.org for debunking fake news.

☐ **Strengthen Password Security**

- Use a password manager like **Bitwarden** or **KeePassXC** to gen-

93

erate and store strong, unique passwords.

- Enable two-factor authentication (2FA) on all accounts.

☐ **Limit Surveillance**

- Turn off location services on your devices unless necessary.

- Regularly audit and delete unused apps and accounts.

- Install **Privacy Badger** to block trackers on your browser.

☐ **Learn and Stay Updated**

- Follow organizations like **EFF** and **Privacy International** to stay informed about digital privacy.

- Regularly review and update your privacy settings across all devices and accounts.

94

What is a VPN & why do all the girlies need one?

A VPN (Virtual Private Network) is a service that creates a secure and encrypted connection between your device and the internet. It routes your internet traffic through a private server—often in another country where privacy laws are strong—hiding your IP address and ensuring your online activities remain private and secure. VPNs are commonly used to:

Enhance Security: Protect sensitive data from hackers, especially on public Wi-Fi.

Bypass Restrictions: Access geo-restricted content like streaming services or blocked websites.

Improve Privacy: Hide your browsing activity from ISPs, advertisers, and government surveillance.

Enable Remote Work: Allow secure access to company networks while working remotely. *

* Caution: if your company provides a VPN for you, it's protecting their privacy, not yours. They have access to your activities and can track whatever you're doing while on the VPN. For your personal security and privacy, you need your own VPN, routed through a country with strict security and privacy laws like Sweden or Switzerland.

How To Choose a VPN Provider

For General Use (Streaming, Privacy, Everyday Security)

NordVPN: Fast, secure, and excellent for streaming (unblocks Netflix, Hulu, BBC iPlayer).

ExpressVPN: Easy to use, very fast, and reliable for bypassing geo-restrictions.

Surfshark: Affordable and allows unlimited devices on one account.

CyberGhost: Great for beginners, with user-friendly apps and streaming-optimized servers.

Recommendation: Choose one of these if you want a solid all-rounder for personal use.

For Advanced Security & Privacy

ProtonVPN: Developed by CERN scientists; focuses on privacy, with a free tier and robust encryption.

Mullvad: No personal account needed–super anonymous and affordable.

IVPN: Excellent for privacy with a strong no-logs policy and advanced security features.

Recommendation: These are ideal for those who prioritize anonymity and privacy.

For Budget-Friendly Options

Surfshark: Best value for money, with excellent features at a low price.

Windscribe (Free or Paid): Generous free plan (10GB/month) and affordable premium options.

AtlasVPN: Affordable with good speeds and essential features.

Recommendation: If cost is a major factor, these are your best bets.

96

How To Configure Your VPN For Maximum Security

1. **Download the VPN Software**
   Go to the official website of your chosen VPN provider or download the app from your device's app store.

2. **Install and Configure**
   - Install the VPN app on your device (computer, smartphone, tablet, etc.).
   - Follow the setup instructions provided by the VPN service.
   - To secure all your online activitie, you must install it on *every connected device*.

3. **Choose the Right Servers**
   - **Use Secure Core Servers:** For the highest level of security, use ProtonVPN's Secure Core servers located in privacy-friendly jurisdictions like Switzerland, Iceland, or Sweden.
   - **Connect to Servers in Privacy-Friendly Countries:** Choose servers in countries with strong privacy laws like Switzerland and Sweden.
   - **Five Eyes** is an intelligence-sharing alliance between five English-speaking countries: United States, United Kingdom, Canada, Australia, New Zealand. *Avoid servers in these countries!*
   - **Avoid High-Traffic Servers:** Check the server

97

load in the app and avoid servers with high traffic for better performance and security.

4. **Test Your VPN**
   Verify it's working by checking your IP address through an online tool like whatismyipaddress. com.

Tips

- Use a Paid VPN** for better speed, reliability, and no data caps.

- Avoid Free VPNs** that monetize your data or show excessive ads.

- Look for Key Features** like a no-logs policy, a kill switch, and multiple server locations.

Additional Considerations

- **Jurisdiction**: Opt for VPNs based in countries with strong privacy laws and outside the jurisdiction of surveillance alliances like the Five Eyes. (

- **Open-Source Software:** VPNs that offer open-source clients allow the community to inspect the code for vulnerabilities, enhancing trust.

- **Independent Audits:** Choose VPNs that have undergone third-party security audits to verify their privacy claims.

- **Obfuscation Features:** Some VPNs offer obfuscation techniques to disguise VPN traffic, making it harder for surveillance entities to detect.

98

While a VPN is a valuable tool for enhancing privacy, it's important to recognize that no solution can guarantee complete anonymity. Combining VPN usage with other privacy practices, such as using encrypted communication tools and maintaining good digital hygiene, will provide a more comprehensive defense against surveillance.

United We Stand: Why Fascism Fears Solidarity

Fascist regimes don't limit their oppression to one demographic—they systematically target diverse groups: minorities, immigrants, LGBTQ+ communities, feminists, journalists, intellectuals, labor unions, and more. The strategy is clear: divide and conquer.

Why It's Important:

Fascism targets everyone

By bringing together all the groups under attack, coalitions create a united front that is too large and diverse to ignore or suppress.

The Civil Rights Movement succeeded because it united Black leaders, religious organizations, students, labor unions, and white allies across the U.S. This coalition brought moral, political, and logistical strength to the fight for equality. "United we stand, divided we fall" serves as a reminder that collaboration is the foundation of success in any collective effort.

The Power of Unity: How the Civil Rights Movement Won Through Coalition-Building

The Civil Rights Movement of the 1950s and 60s wasn't just a single effort by a single group—it was a sprawling, interconnected coalition of diverse voices and organizations, each bringing unique strengths to the fight for racial equality. The story of the 1963 March on Washington for Jobs and Freedom offers a vivid example of how these alliances worked together to achieve lasting change.

101

When people unite across racial, political and ideological lines they can achieve extraordinary things.

The Civil Rights Movement

Not just a moment, but a model for how coalitions can challenge and dismantle oppressive systems.

Story Time

By 1963, the Civil Rights Movement had gained significant momentum, but progress was slow. Black Americans faced systemic racism in education, employment, housing, and voting rights. Violence against activists, such as the murders of Medgar Evers and countless others, underscored the urgency of the movement.

Faced with these challenges, leaders realized they needed a united front to demand federal action. Enter the *March on Washington for Jobs and Freedom,* one of the largest and most iconic demonstrations in American history.

The Coalition Comes Together

The march was not the work of a single organization. It required an extraordinary coalition that brought together groups from across the social and political spectrum, including:

1. **Black Leaders and Civil Rights Organizations**
   Figures like Dr. Martin Luther King Jr. (Southern Christian Leadership Conference), A. Philip Randolph (Brotherhood of Sleeping Car Porters), and John Lewis (Student Nonviolent Coordinating Committee) provided leadership, vision, and

103

moral authority.

2. **Religious Organizations**
Churches and religious leaders played a central
role in organizing the march, mobilizing thousands of participants and framing the fight for
civil rights as a moral imperative. Rabbi Joachim
Prinz, a German refugee from Nazi Germany, was
among the speakers, highlighting the universal
call for justice.

3. **Labor Unions**
A. Philip Randolph, a longtime labor leader,
ensured that unions supported the march, both
financially and logistically. The United Auto Workers (UAW) provided critical funding and helped
organize transportation for protesters.

4. **Student Groups**
The Student Nonviolent Coordinating Committee (SNCC) brought youthful energy, creativity,
and grassroots organizing expertise, ensuring the
march connected with younger generations.

5. **White Allies**
Organizations like the United Federation of
Teachers and individual allies from across the
country joined the march, underscoring the multiracial solidarity behind the movement.

104

_____

The Day of the March

On August 28, 1963, over 250,000 people from all walks of life gathered on the National Mall in Washington, D.C. It was one of the largest demonstrations in U.S. history at the time. Protesters carried signs demanding racial justice, fair wages, voting rights, and an end to segregation.

- **Dr. King's Famous Speech**
  Dr. Martin Luther King Jr.'s **I Have a Dream** speech became the defining moment of the march. While King spoke of a dream for equality, the coalition behind him demonstrated how unity could turn that dream into action.

- **The Results**
  The march placed immense pressure on Congress and President John F. Kennedy, contributing directly to the passage of landmark legislation like the Civil Rights Act of 1964 and the Voting Rights Act of 1965.

_____

Lessons from the Coalition

The success of the March on Washington—and the Civil Rights Movement as a whole—rested on its ability to unite a diverse array of groups, even when they didn't agree on

105

every issue. For example:

- **Strategic Compromise:** Leaders like John Lewis had to tone down fiery rhetoric in his planned speech to align with the broader coalition's goals, demonstrating the importance of finding common ground.

- **Strength in Numbers:** The sheer size and diversity of the march made it impossible for politicians and media to ignore.

The Legacy

The coalition that made the Civil Rights Movement possible offers a timeless lesson: when people unite across racial, political, and ideological lines, they can achieve extraordinary things. The march wasn't just a moment—it was a model for how coalitions can challenge and dismantle oppressive systems.

Strength in Numbers

Fascist regimes thrive on intimidation and fear, making individuals or small groups feel isolated and powerless. A broad coalition offers safety in numbers and the ability to mobilize mass resistance.wasn't just a moment—it was a model for how coalitions can challenge and dismantle oppressive systems.

Why It's Important

When people see a large, united movement, it builds momentum, boosts morale, and encourages others to join the fight. A coalition can organize massive protests, influence public opinion, and push back against authoritarian policies more effectively than fragmented efforts.

Example

The Hong Kong pro-democracy protests brought together students, professionals, religious groups, and the elderly, demonstrating the breadth of support for the movement. This diversity made it harder for the government to dismiss their demands.

107

Diverse Skills and Perspectives

Different groups bring unique experiences, resources, and tactics to a coalition. Workers may organize strikes, students may lead digital campaigns, and religious groups can provide moral authority or safe spaces.

Why It's Important

Fascism exploits societal weaknesses, so a coalition's diversity ensures no single vulnerability can be exploited. Diverse voices also help shape strategies that resonate across communities.

Example

In South Africa's anti-apartheid struggle, coalitions included labor unions, religious organizations, international allies, and youth groups. This diversity allowed the movement to address oppression on multiple fronts—economic, political, and social.

108

The Anti-Apartheid Struggle in South Africa: A Story of Coalition-Building

The fight against apartheid, South Africa's brutal system of institutionalized racial segregation and oppression, was a global and multi-faceted effort. It was a prime example of how diverse coalitions—labor unions, religious organizations, international allies, and youth groups—can come together to dismantle an oppressive system. One key event that demonstrates the power of this coalition is the Congress of the People and the Freedom Charter of 1955.

The Context

By the early 1950s, apartheid policies had stripped Black South Africans of their rights, confining them to segregated areas, denying them political representation, and exploiting them as cheap labor. Resistance efforts, led by organizations like the African National Congress (ANC), were gaining momentum but needed a unifying strategy to bring together the many groups fighting apartheid.

In response, anti-apartheid leaders, including Nelson Mandela and Walter Sisulu, called for a coalition to create a shared vision for a free and democratic South Africa.

The Congress of the People

In 1955, the Congress of the People was organized as a mass gathering to draft a document that would articulate the shared goals of the anti-apartheid movement. The event brought together:

Labor Unions: The South African Congress of Trade Unions (SACTU) represented workers who were striking against unfair wages and labor conditions.

Religious Organizations: Churches and faith leaders mobilized their communities, framing apartheid as a moral injustice that violated human dignity.

110

Youth Groups: The ANC Youth League, spearheaded by future leaders like Nelson Mandela, provided energy and grassroots organizing power.

Women's Organizations: Groups like the Federation of South African Women highlighted the intersection of racial and gender oppression.

International Allies: Support came from outside South Africa, including advocacy groups in the United States, the United Kingdom, and the broader African continent, which amplified the movement's voice on the global stage.

The Congress convened in Kliptown, a township near Johannesburg, and was attended by more than 3,000 delegates representing various racial, social, and political groups. This was groundbreaking in a country where apartheid laws criminalized multiracial gatherings.

The Freedom Charter

The result of the Congress was the **Freedom Charter**, a visionary document that outlined the movement's goals for a free South Africa. It declared that:

- The People Shall Govern!
  All South Africans, regardless of race, would have the right to vote.

- The Land Shall Be Shared Among Those Who Work It!
  Land reform would redistribute wealth and power.

111

- There Shall Be Work and Security! Labor rights, fair wages, and economic opportunities would be guaranteed.
- There Shall Be Peace and Friendship! South Africa would pursue equality and peace at home and abroad.

The Freedom Charter became a rallying cry for the movement, uniting people across class, race, and ideological lines. It also served as the foundation for South Africa's post-apartheid Constitution, adopted in 1996.

Challenges and Crackdowns

The apartheid regime responded to the Congress of the People with brutality. Police raided the event, and leaders were arrested and charged with treason for daring to imagine a multiracial democracy. Despite these attacks, the coalition remained strong. Each group—unions, faith leaders, youth, and international allies—stepped up to sustain the movement when others were silenced or imprisoned.

The Global Coalition

South Africa's anti-apartheid struggle was bolstered by international solidarity:

112

- **Economic Sanctions:** Labor unions in the U.S. and U.K. organized boycotts of South African goods, putting economic pressure on the apartheid government.

- **Cultural Boycotts:** Artists and musicians refused to perform in South Africa, isolating the regime.

- **The Anti-Apartheid Movement:** Advocacy groups around the world raised awareness, lobbied governments, and provided financial and logistical support to activists in South Africa.

The Legacy

The coalition's diversity was its strength. By addressing oppression on multiple fronts—economic, political, and social—the movement built a foundation for sustainable change. The Freedom Charter's vision of equality became a blueprint for the new South Africa after the apartheid regime fell in 1994.

The story of the Congress of the People and the Freedom Charter reminds us that no movement succeeds alone. It takes collaboration, solidarity, and a shared vision to dismantle systemic injustice.

Overcoming Polarization

Fascists fuel division by framing opposition groups as disorganized or at odds with one another. Coalitions counteract this narrative by demonstrating solidarity and common purpose.

Lessons to Remember

Why It's Important

By uniting, groups send a powerful message that their differences are secondary to their shared goal: defeating fascism. This unity builds trust and challenges the regime's attempts to sow discord.

Example

The Women's March (2017) succeeded in bringing together people from across political and social spectrums, creating a visible and united response to authoritarian threats in the U.S.

114

Coalitions allow groups to share resources–funding, platforms, meeting spaces, and media attention– maximizing their collective impact. What one group lacks, another can provide.

Why It's Important

Authoritarian regimes often have vast resources at their disposal, from state propaganda to military force. A coalition pools its strengths to counter this imbalance.

Example

During the resistance to the Dakota Access Pipeline, Native American groups partnered with environmentalists and civil rights organizations, bringing the issue to national and international attention.

115

Increasing Political and Social Pressure

Lessons to Remember

Broad coalitions make it harder for governments to dismiss opposition as fringe or extremist. When different groups with varying ideologies and backgrounds unite, they represent a cross-section of society, making their demands harder to ignore.

Why It's Important

A broad coalition can influence political leaders, pressure corporations, and sway public opinion by showing the regime's unpopularity across demographics.

Example

The anti-Trump resistance movements in the U.S. leveraged coalitions of immigrants, women, LGBTQ+ groups, and labor unions to influence elections and policy debates.

116

Resilience Against Retaliation

Fascist regimes often target specific groups to weaken movements. A coalition makes it harder for them to dismantle opposition, as members can step in to support one another when one group is attacked.

Lessons to Remember

Why It's Important

Solidarity ensures that no group fights alone. When one member is targeted, the rest rally to provide legal, financial, or moral support, keeping the resistance alive.

Example

During the civil rights era, when Black leaders were arrested or assassinated, coalitions ensured that the movement continued, with allies stepping up to fill leadership roles.

117

Together We Are Stronger

Dictators and fascist regimes thrive on division, fear, and isolation. Broad coalitions counter these tactics by building unity, amplifying resistance, and demonstrating the strength of shared purpose. In the fight against authoritarianism, coalitions are not just helpful—they are essential.

The Power of Information: Turning the Tide Against Oppression

Throughout history, the dissemination of information has been a powerful weapon in the hands of the oppressed. From whispered rumors to boldly proclaimed truths, the ability to share stories, ideas, and warnings has not only saved lives but also chipped away at the foundations of authoritarian systems. This chapter examines the ingenious ways people—particularly women—have wielded the power of information as a tool of resistance and how you can use these tools, too.

Even in the darkest times, the smallest actions can lead to profound change.

Irena Sendler

a Polish social worker who used her position—and her wits—to undermine the Nazi regime during World War II.

In the early 1940s, the Nazis established the Warsaw Ghetto, forcing over 400,000 Jewish people into a small, confined space. Disease and starvation were rampant, and the threat of deportation to concentration camps loomed over every family.

Irena Sendler's bravery and ingenuity in rescuing Jewish children during the Holocaust is one of the most extraordinary stories of resistance in history. Her efforts under the guise of a social worker not only saved lives but preserved family identities, ensuring that even in the chaos of war, the bonds of heritage and belonging could someday be restored.

Courage in Plain Sight

As a member of the *Żegota* (Council to Aid Jews), Irena worked tirelessly under the constant threat of death. Her position as a social worker specializing in public health allowed her to secure a permit to

120

enter the Warsaw Ghetto, ostensibly to combat the spread of typhus and other diseases. Nazis were paranoid about epidemics, which gave Irena a rare opportunity to pass in and out of the ghetto without immediate suspicion.

While carrying out her official duties, Irena simultaneously began orchestrating a secret operation to smuggle Jewish children out of the ghetto to safety.

Every trip into the ghetto was an opportunity to save a life. Irena and her network used a variety of ingenious methods to smuggle children past Nazi guards. Infants and small children were placed inside toolboxes, suitcases, or sacks. For older children who could not be concealed in small spaces, Irena utilized ambulances. She instructed her team to feign emergencies, transporting children hidden under stretchers or even in coffins meant to appear as containing victims of typhus.

Some children were hidden beneath garbage in carts being taken out of the ghetto. The stench and the fear of disease deterred guards from inspecting too closely. Irena forged documents to create new identities for the children, often passing them off as orphans or the offspring of Catholic families.

Despite these elaborate methods, every smuggling attempt carried immense risk. If caught, Irena and her collaborators would face immediate execution.

The Power of Gossip and Misdirection

Irena relied on gossip and misdirection to outsmart the Gestapo. She planted rumors about impending typhus outbreaks to deter Nazi soldiers from inspecting certain areas. She leveraged a network of trusted women—nurses, teachers, and housewives—who spread false information to confuse authorities and buy time for her operations.

Every detail mattered. From a strategically timed baby's cry to a forged document, these seemingly small acts were critical in saving lives. Irena's network of women passed messages in flour sacks and sewed maps into clothing. These quiet acts of defiance grew into a larger movement, rescuing over 2,500 Jewish children.

Impact and Recognition

In 1943, Irena was captured and tortured by the Gestapo. Despite enduring unimaginable pain, she refused to reveal the names of her co-conspirators or the children she had saved. Her resilience paid off: members of the Polish underground bribed a guard to secure her release.

Irena's efforts saved approximately 2,500 children. She risked her life daily, enduring arrest, torture, and narrowly escaping execution. Yet her humility shone through in her later years, as she often said, "I could have done more."

In 1965, Irena was recognized as **Righteous Among the Nations** by Yad Vashem, and her story continues to inspire acts of courage and resistance against oppression.

The Ripple Effect of Information

Irena's story highlights the ripple effect of courage. Her actions inspired others to take risks, forming a network of resistance that ultimately saved thousands. The children she rescued grew up to tell her story, ensuring her bravery would not be forgotten.

Key Takeaways from Irena's Story

1. Subtlety is Power: Resistance doesn't always need to be loud. Coded communication and small acts of defiance can have a massive impact.

2. Networks Matter: No one resists alone. Building a trusted network amplifies the effectiveness of resistance.

3. Truth as Legacy: By documenting and preserving information, Irena ensured that the atrocities she witnessed—and the lives she saved—would not be erased by history.

Irine's story serves as a testament to the power of information and the critical role women play in resisting oppression. Her quiet bravery underlines the truth that even in the darkest times, the smallest actions can lead to profound change.

The Power of Subtlety: How to Spread Information Without Detection

1. Coded Messages in the Physical World

Hidden in Plain Sight: In the past, women in the resistance used embroidery, baking patterns, or even recipes to encode messages. A modern woman would incorporate messages into jewelry, clothing, or accessories. For example, using a bracelet with key symbols or colors to notify others that they're part of the underground. IYKYK

Food as Communication: Historical women fighting against fascists baked bread or cookies with designs or shapes that carried hidden meanings. We're still bakers, so go at it! Social media images of these creations can double as a method of spreading the coded message widely.

Ciphers and Symbolism: Employing everyday items (scarves, flowers, or even laundry lines) as covert signals to coordinate actions. Use the placement of household items as signals in a neighborhood. For instance, a blue curtain in a window could indicate a safe house, while a pot of red flowers might signal danger.

Coordinate through everyday objects in shared spaces: a

tilted umbrella or a specific book left on a bench can act as a prearranged signal.

2. Visual Language in the Digital World

Symbolism like certain emojis, colors, or arrangements in social media posts can pass unnoticed by algorithms while carrying significant meaning to those who understand the code.

Share photos with hidden cues, such as specific books, artworks, or plants in the background that indicate messages.

3. Leveraging Playful Language and Memes

Use double entendre, jokes, or wordplay that seem harmless but carry deeper meanings. Humor is an excellent shield against detection while being a potent carrier of truth.

Memes and viral trends can be used to mask dissent, such as turning slogans into catchy, seemingly apolitical phrases with a hidden activist twist.

Encrypted Communication: Apps like Signal or Proton-Mail are essential for private, secure messaging, but even in open forums, use layered codes within images or metadata to share sensitive information.

Hashtag Subversion: Hijack trending hashtags with subtle dissenting content. Pair innocuous posts with coded hashtags to bypass censorship while signaling others to pay attention.

125

4. Channel Your Inner 007 and Gossip Girl!

Authoritarian regimes thrive on fear and control. Gossip is a powerful, decentralized tool to disseminate alternative narratives. Strategies include:

Whisper Networks: Passing information at markets, in salons, or at church gatherings. Keep your communication offline and in-person so it's not intercepted.

Humor & Ridicule: Undermining authority by turning powerful figures into the butt of jokes. Rather than passing along stories that make the oppressors scary, refer to them as silly, or weird.

Personal Stories: Sharing first-hand accounts to humanize victims of oppression and inspire action, either in person or online. The reverse of this, *don't* share the memes and stories the oppressors want passed around. Starve them of attention oxygen.

126

The Mothers of the Plaza de Mayo: Silent Defiance That Shook a Regime

In the late 1970s, Argentina was in the grip of a brutal military dictatorship. Under the guise of maintaining order, the regime abducted tens of thousands of people—students, activists, journalists, and everyday citizens—branding them as subversives. These individuals became *los desaparecidos*—the disappeared. They were taken from their homes, schools, and streets, never to be seen again.

For most Argentinians, fear silenced them. Speaking out risked becoming the next victim. But for a group of grieving mothers, silence became a powerful tool of defiance.

Key Takeaways

The Strength of Symbols: The white scarves became a universally recognized emblem of their cause, proving that even small, simple symbols can inspire massive movements.

Persistence as Protest: By showing up every week, no matter the threat, the mothers demonstrated that resistance is not always about grand gestures—it's about unwavering commitment.

Global Attention as Leverage: Their quiet defiance drew the eyes of the world, pressuring the regime and giving the movement allies beyond Argentina.

127

How the Movement Began

The first gathering was modest: a small group of mothers whose children had disappeared went to the Plaza de Mayo, the central square in Buenos Aires, to demand answers from the government. They wore white scarves—symbolizing the cloth diapers of their missing children—and walked silently in a circle around the square.

The dictatorship had silenced political dissent, but it hadn't prepared for this unique rebellion. These were not activists or radicals; they were mothers, women whose identities and grievances were rooted in their roles as caregivers and protectors. Their message was simple and devastating: *Where are our children?*

The Power of Presence and Silence

The Plaza de Mayo was a carefully controlled public space, often used by the regime for grand displays of power. The sight of these mothers—clad in white scarves, walking in silence—turned this symbol of authority into a stage for resistance.

The silence of the mothers spoke louder than any slogan or chant. It symbolized the void left by their missing children and defied the gov-

128

ernment's narrative that the disappeared were merely criminals or traitors. Their white scarves became a potent symbol of hope, grief, *and resistance.*

Escalating Risks

As the mothers gained visibility, so too did the risks. The regime labeled them as agitators, accusing them of spreading lies and collaborating with subversives. Many of the mothers were harassed, threatened, or even arrested. In a chilling twist, some mothers themselves were disappeared for speaking out.

But their numbers grew. Week after week, more mothers joined the marches. Their persistence drew international attention, shattering the regime's carefully constructed image of control and exposing its human rights violations to the world.

The Mothers of the Plaza de Mayo remind us that resistance can take many forms, and that even the smallest acts—like walking in a circle—can challenge the most oppressive systems. Their courage serves as an enduring lesson: love and grief are not just emotions; they can be forces of profound change.

129

Resistance can take many forms.
Even the smallest acts can challenge the most oppressive systems.

What a Girl's Gotta Know

The unique power of women-led resistance, shows how grief and love can be transformed into tools for justice.

Guerrilla Tactics: Loud, Visible Resistance

In the face of authoritarian control, sometimes subtlety isn't enough—bold, visible acts of defiance become essential to inspire, disrupt, and dismantle oppressive systems. Guerrilla tactics are the embodiment of loud resistance, combining creativity and courage to challenge power in unexpected ways.

From graffiti that reclaims public spaces to flash mobs that erupt in moments of coordinated chaos, these tactics make oppression impossible to ignore. They disrupt the narratives of regimes, amplify the voices of the marginalized, and often come with immense personal risk.

Bold actions—grounded in ingenuity and solidarity—become sparks that ignite larger movements for freedom and justice.

Public Art and Protest

Graffiti as a tool for dissent: From Banksy-style messaging to slogans like "Who killed Kian?" in the Philippines,

131

visible art disrupts controlled narratives.

Graffiti and murals, often created in public spaces, amplify the voices of the marginalized and challenge government propaganda. Messages like **"Who killed Kian?"**–referring to a teenager killed during Duterte's controversial war on drugs–transformed walls into protest banners, forcing the public to confront uncomfortable truths. These artworks bypass traditional media, giving people a means to express dissent and create solidarity in ways that are immediate, impactful, and impossible to ignore.

Hijacking Media

- **Intercepting Radio Signals:** During apartheid in South Africa, pirate radio broadcasts became a lifeline for resistance, spreading messages of hope, solidarity, and defiance in a time of extreme censorship. Stations like **Radio Freedom**, run by the African National Congress (ANC), broadcasted from neighboring countries, sharing revolutionary songs, speeches, and news that countered the state's propaganda.

  These clandestine broadcasts gave voice to the oppressed, kept the spirit of resistance alive, and connected disparate communities fighting for freedom. Despite the government's attempts to jam signals, the broadcasts persisted, proving that even in the darkest times, the power of communication can unite and inspire.

132

- **Social Media Waves:** Social media has become a battlefield for resistance, where orchestrated viral campaigns can expose regime vulnerabilities and amplify calls for change. From hashtags like ***#EndSARS*** in Nigeria to **#MilkTeaAlliance** uniting pro-democracy movements in Asia, these digital movements leverage global attention to pressure authoritarian governments.

  Viral videos, memes, and coordinated posts not only raise awareness of human rights abuses but also rally international support, undermining the regimes' attempts to control narratives. By turning platforms designed for connection into tools for accountability, these campaigns prove that the digital age offers new and powerful ways to challenge oppression.

Everyday Defiance

- **Refusing Conformity:** Small acts of disobedience, like wearing banned colors or playing forbidden music, become quiet yet potent forms of resistance under authoritarian regimes. These seemingly simple actions challenge the illusion of total control, signaling defiance and solidarity among the oppressed.

  Each act, though small, carries immense symbolic weight, showing that even under severe repression, the human spirit cannot be fully subdued. Over time, these

133

collective acts of defiance chip away at the regime's authority, inspiring others to join in and proving that resistance can thrive even in the face of oppression.

- **Organized Flash Mobs:** Organized flash mobs have been used effectively in places like Hong Kong during the pro-democracy protests, where quick, impactful demonstrations became a hallmark of the resistance. Protesters would gather suddenly in public spaces to chant slogans, sing songs, or hold symbolic actions, then disperse before authorities could react.

This tactic minimized the risk of arrest while maximizing visibility, disrupting the government's control of public spaces. Flash mobs demonstrated the adaptability and coordination of modern resistance movements, turning spontaneity into a strategic advantage against authoritarian surveillance and repression.

MODERN DAY

Resistance Checklist

In the digital age, modern tools and technologies have revolution-
ized the ways people resist authoritarian regimes, offering new av-
enues for organizing, communicating, and spreading awareness.

☐ *Encrypted Communication Apps:* Platforms like
    Signal, Telegram, and WhatsApp have become
    lifelines for activists and organizers. Protesters use
    these platforms to coordinate meeting points,
    share safety updates, and disseminate real-time
    information without fear of interception.

☐ *QR Codes for Information Dissemination:* Activists
    embed these codes in posters, stickers, or street
    art, leading to websites, videos, or encrypted
    platforms that provide accurate information about
    government abuses or upcoming protests. These
    codes are easy to distribute, difficult to trace, and
    accessible to anyone with a smartphone, making
    them a low-risk method to bypass censorship and
    reach broader audiences..

☐ *Harnessing Social Media for International Solidar-
    ity:* The interconnectedness of the modern world

135

allows local struggles to gain global traction. Activists use platforms like Mastodon, Bluesky, and TikTok to share stories, videos, and live updates, attracting international attention and solidarity.

- ☐ **Crowdsourced Resistance Tools:** Protesters have developed open-source tools and maps to enhance safety and efficiency. For example, during the Hong Kong protests, demonstrators used live maps to track police movements and identify safe zones. These tools often rely on real-time input from participants, creating a decentralized but highly effective system of organization.

- ☐ **Decentralized Media and Livestreaming:** Livestreaming through platforms like YouTube or Periscope enables activists to document events as they happen, providing unfiltered evidence of government actions. This not only bypasses state-controlled media but also holds regimes accountable by sharing the truth with a global audience.

- ☐ **Crowdfunding and Crypto for Financial Independence:** Traditional financial systems can be weaponized by authoritarian regimes to cut off funding for resistance movements. Activists increasingly turn to crowdfunding platforms and cryptocurrencies to sustain their activities. Blockchain technology ensures that funds remain secure, transparent, and beyond the reach of government interference.

By combining traditional resistance tactics with these modern tools, activists and ordinary citizens alike are finding innovative ways to stand up against oppression, proving that technology can be a powerful equalizer in the fight for freedom and justice.

Substitute Platforms for Protesters

Since Twitter has shifted under Elon Musk's ownership it is no longer safe and reliable for activists, protesters, and marginalized groups. Alternative platforms and strategies have emerged as substitutes for organizing, communicating, and amplifying dissent. *But remember, this may change as authoritarian regimes infiltrate and further control communication platforms.*

137

Social Media Platforms You Can Trust (for now)

Here are some prefered options which, at the time of this writing, have more privacy, security, and independence from centralized control:

1. Mastodon
(Decentralized and Open-Source)

A federated social network where users can create or join servers based on shared interests or regions. Its decentralized nature makes it resistant to central control or censorship. Protesters can create private instances or join activist-focused ones for safer communication.

2. Bluesky
(Decentralized Alternative from Twitter's Co-Founder)

While still in development, Bluesky emphasizes decentralization and user control over algorithms. Its open protocol allows for diverse moderation options and increased user autonomy, making it a promising alternative for activists.

3. Signal
(Encrypted Messaging and Group Communication)

Originally a private messaging app, Signal now supports group chats and communities, making it a secure option for organizing and sharing real-time updates. Its privacy features and end-to-end encryption make it a favorite among activists.

4. Telegram
(Channels and Large Groups)

Known for its channels and large group chats, Telegram allows activists to broadcast messages to thousands of followers. It supports anonymity and provides tools like self-destructing messages, but users should be cautious of its potential vulnerabilities in certain regimes.

138

5. Matrix

(Decentralized and Encrypted Communication)

An open-source, decentralized messaging protocol that supports apps like Element. It offers secure and private communication for individuals and groups, making it ideal for activists seeking alternatives to centralized platforms.

6. Reddit

(Community-Based Discussions)

While not as secure for organizing sensitive actions, Reddit remains a popular platform for discussions and raising awareness through activist-focused subreddits (e.g., r/activism, r/protest). Protesters can use pseudonyms and private subreddits for more security.

7. Diaspora

(Decentralized and User-Owned Social Media)

A non-commercial, federated social network where users own their data. It operates similarly to Mastodon, with user-controlled servers called "pods."

8. TikTok

(Creative and Viral Messaging)

Although it comes with surveillance risks, TikTok's ability to make ideas go viral can be leveraged to spread awareness quickly. Activists can use the platform for coded messaging and cultural disruption while being cautious about personal information.*

As of this writing, TikTok is scheduled to be banned in the US early 2025. See the chapter on setting up a VPN if you're in America and still want to use it.

Profiles in Courage: Women Who Outsmarted Regimes

Learn more about amazing girls and women who did not cower in the face of fascist regimes and oppressors.

Malala Yousafzai (Pakistan)

Born in Pakistan's Swat Valley, Malala Yousafzai grew up under the oppressive rule of the Taliban, who banned girls' education. Refusing to be silenced, Malala began speaking out, blogging for the BBC and appearing in local media to advocate for girls' right to learn. At just 15, she survived an assassination attempt by a Taliban gunman, a moment that catapulted her story onto the global stage. Rather than succumbing to fear, Malala transformed her personal tragedy into a worldwide movement for education, becoming the youngest-ever Nobel Peace Prize laureate. Through her foundation,

140

she continues to empower girls to fight for their right to education in the face of systemic oppression.

Phoolan Devi (India)

 Phoolan Devi's life was a tale of defiance against India's entrenched caste system and patriarchal norms. Born into a low-caste family, she endured systemic abuse and violence before taking up arms and becoming a feared bandit queen. Leading a gang that targeted oppressive landowners and those who had wronged her, Phoolan became a folk hero to India's marginalized. After surrendering and serving time in prison, she reinvented herself as a politician, winning a seat in Parliament. Her journey from victim to outlaw to leader symbolizes resilience and rebellion against deeply rooted systems of injustice.

Tsitsi Dangarembga (Zimbabwe)

Renowned author and filmmaker Tsitsi Dangarembga has used her voice to critique Zimbabwe's corruption and human rights abuses. Known for her acclaimed novel *Nervous Conditions*, she combines artistic expression with activism, highlighting the struggles of women in post-colonial Africa. In 2020, Tsitsi was arrested for staging a solitary, peaceful protest against government corruption, holding a placard that read, "We want better. Reform our institutions." Her quiet courage in the face of authoritarian oppression underscores the power of intellectual and moral defiance, proving that even a single voice can inspire resistance.

Call to Action
What You Can Do

Everyday resistance is about subtle, sustainable actions that challenge authoritarian systems without putting oneself in immediate danger. It's the quiet but persistent defiance woven into daily life: sharing truthful information in private conversations, supporting local businesses instead of state-controlled ones, or wearing symbols of dissent that go unnoticed by authorities but resonate within the community.

It's using humor to undermine oppressive narratives, spreading memes that ridicule power, or amplifying voices of dissent through anonymous social media accounts. Everyday resistance doesn't require grand gestures; it's about finding safe, creative ways to undermine control, maintain solidarity, and nurture hope, proving that even small acts can contribute to a larger movement for change.

143

Safeguarding Yourself & Building Your Freedom Squad

When fascism is on the rise, protecting yourself online and in real life becomes not just a matter of personal security but a form of resistance. Authoritarian regimes and their supporters often weaponize surveillance and public information against those who dissent. Your digital footprint—social media posts, location data, even casual online conversations—can be exploited to track your movements, intimidate you, or undermine your efforts.

Protecting yourself online is the foundation of modern-day safety, especially in turbulent times

By taking steps to secure your online presence, you protect not only yourself but also your community (Mom, Dad, Sis, your besties, that girl in class that you wish were your bestie). Digital safety practices like using encrypted messaging, limiting public visibility of your social media, and recognizing phishing attempts are essential tools for maintaining autonomy and resisting oppressive forces.

In the physical world, the risks are equally significant. Protesters and activists may face heightened scrutiny, targeted harassment, or even physical violence. Governments or extremist groups may monitor public spaces, infiltrate community networks, and exploit moments of vulnerability.

Ensuring your safety by being aware of your surroundings, building escape plans, and connecting with trusted allies can mean the difference between feeling powerless and reclaiming your agency. Protecting yourself is not about fear—it's about creating the resilience and strength needed to stand firm in the face of oppression and safeguard your ability to continue fighting for justice.

Online Protection

As we explored in depth in **"Chapter 6: How to Keep Your Secrets"** protecting yourself online is the foundation of modern-day safety, especially in turbulent times. From mastering digital hygiene to safeguarding your communications with encryption and pseudonyms, these practices are your first line of defense against surveillance and bad actors.

If you haven't already, revisit that chapter for a comprehensive guide to securing your digital presence—it's an essential read before diving into the broader strategies for protecting yourself in real life and building resilient networks of support. Now, grab the checklist below and give it a once-over to make sure you're locked, loaded, and ready to roll.

THE CHECK LISTS

Start with Digital Hygien

- ☐ Use strong, unique passwords with a password manager.

- ☐ Enable two-factor authentication (2FA) on all accounts.

- ☐ Regularly update software and devices to patch vulnerabilities.

- ☐ Be cautious with links and email attachments—verify before clicking.

146

Privacy as Power

☐ Adjust your social media privacy settings to limit visibility to friends and trusted connections. And be scrupulous—ask yourself, *Is Joe really my friend? How do I even know him?* If he's not inner circle, it might be time for Joe to enjoy your content from the sidelines—or not at all.

☐ Avoid oversharing personal details that could compromise your security—like your location, financial info, or anything that screams *"track me!"* Think twice before posting that picture of your morning coffe that just so happens to include your backyard fence or the sign for your local dog park. Keep them guessing, not following.

☐ Use encrypted communication tools like Signal for sensitive conversations. Signal is safe because it uses end-to-end encryption, meaning only you and the person you're chatting with can see the messages—no one else, not even Signal itself. It doesn't store your chat history on its servers and keeps your data private, unlike many mainstream apps that collect and sell your information. Plus, it's open-source, so its security practices are transparent and regularly vetted by experts.

147

Advanced Safety Tactics

- ☐ Use VPNs to protect your online activity, especially on public Wi-Fi.

- ☐ Familiarize yourself with phishing and scams to spot red flags.

- ☐ Consider pseudonymous profiles for activism or other sensitive activities.

Phishing for Dissent: How Scams Target Protestors and Undermine Resistance

Phishing & scams are more than just annoying emails promising you a cut of a prince's fortune—they're sophisticated tools often used to infiltrate, track, and manipulate people. These tactics rely on deception to trick you into revealing sensitive information, such as passwords, financial details, or even personal opinions that could expose you to harm. In the wrong hands, this information can be weaponized to monitor, discredit, or silence dissent, especially in politically charged environments.

For example, phishing emails have been used to target activists and protestors by mimicking trusted organizations or individuals. A common tactic is to send an email appearing to come from a fellow activist, asking for login details to a shared document or account. Once the attacker gains access, they can exploit the information to dismantle networks, leak sensitive data, or identify individuals for targeted harassment or arrest.

In Action: Real-World Examples

During the 2020 Belarus protests, reports emerged of phishing campaigns targeting activists using fake messages from supposed supporters or international organizations. These scams were designed to gather information about protest organizers, which was then used by authorities to track, detain, and intimidate individuals.

149

 Even more alarming, phishing has been used to inject malware into activists' devices, turning their phones into surveillance tools. In Hong Kong, for instance, activists received links in WhatsApp messages that installed spyware capable of monitoring their calls, texts, and locations, exposing their entire networks to risk.

How to Protect Yourself

Be skeptical of unsolicited messages, even from seemingly trustworthy sources. Never click on links or download attachments without verifying their authenticity—double-check URLs, ask the sender directly through a different communication channel, and stay cautious. If it looks suspicious, it probably is. Scams prey on urgency and trust, so staying vigilant is one of your strongest defenses.

Guarding Yourself in the Physical World

When the stakes are high, protecting yourself in the real world becomes just as crucial as safeguarding your online presence. Whether you're attending a protest, navigating public spaces, or simply living your day-to-day life, staying safe requires awareness, preparation, and a strong network of allies.

This section is your guide to physical security—because when you're standing up for what's right, your safety is non-negotiable.

150

Staying Safe IRL

Protecting Your Physical Space

☐ Secure your home with modern locks, security cameras, and alarms.

☐ Have a "go-bag" ready for emergencies (include essentials like ID, cash, medicine, and a backup phone).

Situational Awareness

☐ Stay aware of your surroundings and trust your instincts.

☐ Know the nearest exits in public places and keep a mental plan for emergencies.

Legal and Financial Protections

☐ Keep important documents secure but accessible in case of evacuation.

☐ Stay informed about your rights in protests or public spaces.

☐ Build an emergency fund to cover unexpected costs.

151

GRAB-AND-GO ESSENTIALS:

Your Emergency Exit Kit

Here's what to pack in your **go-bag** to ensure you're ready for anything, whether you're heading to a protest, evacuating during a crisis, or needing to stay mobile on short notice:

The Essentials:

☐ Identification: Driver's license, passport, or any government-issued ID. Keep copies of these, too (physical or encrypted digital).

☐ Cash: Small bills in a waterproof pouch—ATMs might not be an option.

☐ Medicine: A 7-day supply of any prescription medications, plus over-the-counter basics like pain relievers, antacids, and allergy meds.

☐ Important legal documents: Store them in a waterproof, fireproof pouch and include both originals and copies. For extra security, back them up digitally in an encrypted cloud storage or on a secure USB drive.

Communication:

☐ Backup Phone: A prepaid burner phone with minutes loaded.

☐ Chargers: Include a portable power bank and charging cables.

☐ Notebook and Pen: Analog tools are always handy, especially if devices fail.

Safety Gear:

☐ Face Mask or Bandana: For anonymity or tear gas protection.

☐ First Aid Kit: Bandages, antiseptic wipes, and trauma supplies.

☐ Emergency Whistle: To signal for help if needed.

Comfort and Sustainability:

☐ Water: A reusable bottle and/or purification tablets.

☐ Snacks: High-energy, non-perishable foods like granola bars or nuts.

☐ Clothing: Weather-appropriate layers, socks, and a compact rain poncho.

Documentation and Tools:

☐ Emergency Contacts: Written list of phone numbers for trusted people and legal aid.

153

- ☐ Map: A physical map of the area, especially if GPS is unavailable.

- ☐ Multi-tool: A compact tool for cutting, opening, or repairing.

Extras for Protestors:

- ☐ Protective Gear: Goggles or shatterproof glasses to shield against tear gas or debris.

- ☐ Legal Aid Info: Write down the contact info for local lawyers or bail funds.

- ☐ Backup Plan Notes: Routes, safe meeting spots, and secondary escape options.

A well-packed go-bag isn't just a kit—it's peace of mind. Tailor it to your personal needs, and make sure it's easy to grab at a moment's notice.

154

Building Networks of Mutual Aid

What is Mutual Aid?

Mutual aid is a grassroots system where community members come together to support one another through the exchange of resources, skills, and time. Unlike charity, which often operates with a top-down structure, mutual aid is built on reciprocity and solidarity. It's not about helping from a place of pity—it's about recognizing our interconnectedness and creating systems where everyone has what they need to thrive.

Why it Matters

Mutual aid is vital, especially when institutions falter or fail to meet the needs of the people they're meant to serve. By pooling resources and knowledge, mutual aid networks create safety nets that are nimble and community-driven, filling gaps where traditional systems can't— or won't. In times of crisis, whether it's a natural disaster, political upheaval, or systemic breakdown, mutual aid fosters resilience by ensuring that no one faces challenges alone. It's a testament to the power of collective action and the strength of community.

155

A Freedom Squad is more than just a group of friends—it's a trusted network of individuals who share your values, have your back, and are committed to mutual support in both everyday life and times of crisis.

Finding Your Freedom Squad

The ideal squad brings together people with diverse skills and strengths:

- **Emotional Support:** Friends who provide encouragement and a safe space to process emotions.

- **Technical Knowledge:** Individuals with skills in technology, logistics, or communication tools.

- **Legal Expertise:** Allies who understand the law and can advise or connect you with resources.

- **Practical Problem-Solvers:** People who can help with transportation, childcare, or other logistical needs during emergencies.

This mix ensures your squad is well-rounded and equipped to handle challenges from multiple angles, whether it's organizing a neighborhood effort or responding to a sudden crisis.

How to Build Your Squad

Finding your Freedom Squad requires intention, action, and a willingness to build trust over time. Here's how to start:

- **Show Up in Your Community:** Attend local events, protests, meetups, or volunteer opportunities. These are great places to meet like-minded people who share your values and are already engaged.

- **Leverage Online Communities:** Join forums, social media groups, or apps dedicated to causes and interests you care about. Look for opportunities to collaborate or connect on shared goals.

- **Be Proactive:** Don't wait for others to make the first move. Offer help, start a conversation, or invite someone to collaborate on a project. Mutual aid starts with mutual effort.

- **Vet Potential Members:** Trust is key, so take time to get to know people before inviting them into your inner circle. Watch how they show up for others and assess their reliability before including them in sensitive matters.

Ways to Strengthen Bonds

Once you've found your Freedom Squad, it's essential to nurture those relationships to keep the group strong and cohesive.

158

- **Regular Check-Ins:** Schedule informal meet-ups, group calls, or potlucks to stay connected. These moments foster trust and build a sense of belonging.

- **Collaborate on Shared Projects:** Working together on tangible goals, like a co-op garden, skill-sharing workshops, or a neighborhood watch, helps solidify trust and teamwork.

- **Create Emergency Plans:** Establish clear communication channels (e.g., group chats, phone trees) and agree on meeting points or action plans for various scenarios. Knowing you can rely on each other during a crisis is key to your squad's effectiveness.

- **Celebrate Wins Together:** Whether big or small, take time to acknowledge accomplishments or milestones within your group. Celebrations strengthen bonds and keep morale high.

Building a Freedom Squad is about more than safety—it's about creating a community that sustains and uplifts you in both challenging and everyday moments. With the right people by your side, you'll be better prepared for whatever comes your way.

Resource Sharing: Building Collective Security

In times of political instability and rising authoritarianism, resource sharing becomes a lifeline for those resisting oppression or simply trying to survive. By pooling your community's resources, you reduce dependence on unreliable systems and ensure everyone has access to what they need.

Establish a Tool-Sharing Network Create a local or digital inventory of items essential for survival or resistance, such as camping gear, first aid kits, communication devices, and tools for repairs. Use secure platforms to coordinate borrowing and lending while maintaining privacy.

Organize Underground Supply Drives Distribute essential goods like food, warm clothing, hygiene products, or protective gear (masks, goggles, gloves) to vulnerable community members or protestors. Coordinate discreetly to avoid drawing attention from authorities or antagonistic groups.

Share Safe Transportation Set up a system for transporting people or supplies under the radar. This could include offering rides to protests, providing escape routes, or ferrying supplies to those in hiding or isolated.

Skill Swaps: Building Collective Strength

Teach Survival Skills

Offer and trade practical skills like first aid, self-defense, encryption, or basic mechanics. For example, someone knowledgeable in digital security could train others in protecting their devices, while a medic could teach emergency wound care.

Host Covert Workshops

Organize small, trusted gatherings to train members of your group in critical areas such as organizing resistance efforts, navigating check-points, or de-escalating dangerous situations. Use word-of-mouth or secure channels to spread the word.

Develop Community Experts

Build long-term mentorships to pass on expertise that may be harder to acquire under repressive conditions, such as legal rights training, food preservation, or stealth communication techniques.

EMERGENCY PREPAREDNESS TOGETHER

Staying One Step Ahead

In a fascist regime, emergencies can range from sudden police crackdowns to targeted harassment or mass displacement. Preparing as a group ensures no one is left behind and builds resilience in the face of systemic oppression.

162

What You Can Do

- **Secure Communication Networks:** Set up encrypted group chats on platforms like Signal for quick coordination during raids, protests, or sudden evacuations. Use phone trees as a backup for those without access to secure devices.

- **Map Resources and Safe Houses:** Identify and discreetly document critical resources like medical facilities, food storage sites, and allies' homes that can serve as shelters or meeting points. Ensure this information is tightly controlled to prevent infiltration.

- **Practice Evasion and Response Scenarios:** Run drills for dispersing from protests, avoiding surveillance, or responding to raids. For instance, simulate an escape from a compromised location, coordinating through your secure communication network.

- **Stockpile and Hide Essentials:** Work together to gather emergency supplies, such as food, water, medicine, and protective gear, and store them in hidden locations. Share the locations only with trusted members to prevent them from being confiscated.

By sharing resources, swapping survival-critical skills, and preparing for emergencies collectively, your group becomes a self-sufficient and resilient force in the face of authoritarian threats. This isn't just about survival—it's about protecting each other, resisting oppression, and creating the infrastructure to endure and fight back.

Maintaining Balance & Growth

Avoid Burnout in Activism and Mutual Aid

Listen, saving the world is exhausting work, and burnout is the sneaky villain waiting to zap your energy when you least expect it. If you're going to be a badass freedom fighter, you need to protect your time, your energy, and your sanity like they're state secrets. Staying in the fight means knowing when to hit pause, recharge, and pass the baton. Let's get into it.

Set Boundaries: Don't Be a Martyr

You can't save the day if you're running on fumes. Setting boundaries is how you keep your superpowers intact.

- **Know Your Limits:** Be honest about what you can do and what you can't. If your

165

schedule is already packed tighter than a protester's go-bag, it's okay to say, ***"Sorry, I'm tapped out this week."*** Overextending yourself doesn't make you a hero—it makes you tired.

- **Learn the Power of No:** Saying no isn't just okay—it's revolutionary. Don't feel guilty for protecting your energy. If it's not your lane or your load, let someone else carry it.

- **Respect Everyone's Bubble:** In your Freedom Squad, boundaries are sacred. No guilt-tripping, no pushing people past their comfort zones. Consent is queen.

- **Delegate Like a Boss:** You don't have to be a one-person resistance. Share the work, trust your team, and let others step up. Mutual aid is a team sport, not a solo mission. Organize small, trusted gatherings to train members of your group in critical areas such as organizing resistance efforts, navigating checkpoints, or de-escalating dangerous situations. Use word-of-mouth or secure channels to spread the word.

Take Time for Self-Care: Recharge Your Superpowers

Burnout doesn't just knock on the door—it kicks it in if you don't take care of yourself. Self-care isn't indulgent; it's how you stay in the fight.

- **Do What Fills Your Tank:** Whether it's yoga, painting, binging old-school *Buffy* episodes, or dancing like no one's watching, find what recharges you and make it a non-negotiable part of your week.

- **Unleash Your Creative Side:** Write, draw, sing, scream into a void—whatever gets those emotions out. Creative outlets not only heal, but they're also great tools for activism. Protest signs don't design themselves.

- **Reconnect with Your 'Why':** When the grind gets tough, remind yourself why you're doing this. Maybe it's for your besties, your community, or just to stick it to the man—whatever it is, keep it front and center.

- **Unplug When You Need To:** Doomscrolling isn't helping anyone. Step away from the news or social media if it's frying your nerves. Trust us, the world will still be spinning when you get back.

Remember: You're Not Alone

Burnout loves isolation, so don't go it alone. Lean on your Freedom Squad, vent when you need to, and celebrate your wins—even the little ones, like finally getting everyone in the group chat to agree on a meeting time. Remember: it's not just about surviving; it's about thriving.

So, take care of yourself, set those boundaries like a pro, and remember—you're no good to the movement if you're burnt out. Rest isn't a luxury; it's a revolutionary act. Stay fierce, stay focused, and keep fighting the good fight.

Growing & Sustaining the Movement

Movements don't just happen—they're built, nurtured, and passed down like heirloom recipes for justice. To survive and thrive in the long haul, you've got to think beyond the here and now. Building a movement that outlasts you means bringing in fresh faces, keeping things adaptable, and knowing when to shake things up. Here's how to keep the fire burning for generations to come.

169

Adapt and Innovate: Bring Your New Ideas to the Fight

The fight needs you—not just your energy but your fresh ideas, your unique perspective, and your fearless drive to question the way things have always been done. Movements only grow stronger when new voices step up and shake things up. Don't hold back—your creativity and innovation are exactly what's needed to take the resistance to the next level.

Ask the Hard Questions:

If something doesn't make sense, call it out. Why are we still using this outdated tactic? Could we be organizing better? Your perspective is valuable because you're coming in with fresh eyes. Don't be afraid to ask *"What if we tried this instead?"* That's how change happens.

170

Introduce New Tools and Tech:

You know what's trending, what's cutting-edge, and how to use it. Maybe it's organizing through a secure app, making viral TikToks that educate, or using AI tools to outsmart surveillance. Whatever it is, your tech-savvy skills can help the movement stay one step ahead.

Challenge the Status Quo:

Just because "we've always done it this way" doesn't mean it's the best way. Your ideas—no matter how wild or unconventional they seem—could be the game-changer the fight needs. Bring them to the table, pitch them to the squad, and don't be discouraged if not everyone gets it right away. Change takes time, and you're here to push boundaries.

171

Collaborate, Don't Conform:

Share your ideas with your team, but remember, movements are about working together. Pair your innovation with the wisdom of those who've been in the fight for a while. Together, you can build something unstoppable.

This fight is yours as much as anyone else's, and it's your ideas that will keep it moving forward. Don't be afraid to take risks, think big, and do things differently. The revolution needs your creativity, your boldness, and your fresh perspective—so step up and show the world what you've got.

Keep the
Momentum Alive

Movements don't sustain themselves—they thrive because of your passion, your persistence, and your ability to adapt. **You** are the fresh voice, the next leader, the one who will take this fight further than we ever could. The goal isn't just to keep the fire burning—it's to make it an unstoppable blaze.

Stay flexible, stay curious, and always push for better. The revolution isn't a moment; it's a marathon, and you're the one carrying the baton. Keep running—you've got this.

173

Section 1: When to Stay and Fight

In life, there are moments to dig in, fight for what's yours, and stand your ground. But equally important is recognizing when the battle is lost, the cost is too high, or the timing simply isn't right. This chapter is your guide to making that call and executing it like a pro.

Knowing when to run isn't about cowardice—it's about survival, strategy, and seizing a better opportunity elsewhere.

Choosing to stay and fight is not a decision to be taken lightly. It requires clarity, courage, and a deep understanding of what's truly at stake. Here's how to identify when standing your ground is the right move—and how to prepare for the challenges ahead.

When to Stand Firm

There's nowhere to run, but there's also nowhere better

to make a stand than where you are. History shows that some of the most transformative moments come when people decide to fight back, not because it's easy, but because it's necessary.

Rosa Parks refused to give up her bus seat, sparking a national civil rights movement.

Hong Kong Protesters faced tear gas, arrests, and worse to demand democracy.

Lech Wałęsa led labor strikes in Poland that eventually toppled a communist regime.

These are people who didn't wait for the perfect time or place. They fought where they stood—and changed the world because of it.

Deciding to stay and fight isn't about diving in recklessly. It's about being intentional, assessing risks, and knowing when the cause is truly worth it. A wise warrior chooses their battles—and ensures they're equipped to win. When the stakes are personal, your resources are solid, or the fight is unavoidable, plant your feet firmly and face the challenge with strategy and determination.

ASK YOURSELF THESE THREE QUESTIONS

1. Are the Stakes Personal?

Sometimes, the stakes hit close to home. These are the battles where walking away would mean compromising on your values, letting down those you care about, or losing something irreplaceable. Fighting isn't just an option here—it's a necessity.

Examples:

- Defending a loved one from harm, whether physical, emotional, or reputational.

- Standing up for your beliefs in the face of discrimination or unfair treatment.

- Protecting your intellectual property or work from theft or exploitation.

How to Prepare:

- Clearly define what you're fighting for and why it matters. This clarity will help you stay resilient under pressure.

- Rally support from those who share your values or have a vested interest in the outcome.

2. Do I Have the Advantage?

When it comes to fighting a dictator, it's not about charging in headfirst with nothing but righteous anger—you need strategy, resources, and an edge. If you've got the tools, the allies, or the momentum to tip the scales, it's time to seriously consider standing your ground and making your move. Fighting smart is just as important as

176

fighting hard.

- **Do I have leverage?** Whether it's access to critical information, international backing, or a platform to amplify the truth, assess what you bring to the fight.

- **Are there allies who can stand with me?** Dictatorships thrive on isolation. If you can rally others–whether it's grassroots organizers, whistleblowers, or international human rights groups–you're already in a stronger position.

- **What's the cost of this fight?** Be honest about the risks. Are you ready to face personal danger, loss, or retaliation? And is the potential reward– a freer, fairer future–worth that price?

Examples of Advantage

- **Coordinated Resistance:** You're part of a strong movement with a clear plan and widespread support, like the pro-democracy protests in Belarus led by Sviatlana Tsikhanouskaya.

- **International Attention:** You've captured the world's focus, as Hong Kong activists did during their fight for autonomy, using media and global solidarity to expose the regime's abuses.

- **Strategic Disruption:** You have inside knowledge or resources to undermine the regime's infrastructure–think whistleblowers who expose

177

corruption or workers who organize strikes to disrupt the state's machinery.

3. Is There Anywhere to Run?

Sometimes you stay because you have no other options. If the walls are closing in and the exits are blocked, the only option left is to turn and face the problem head-on. When you're up against a dictatorship or oppressive system, running away isn't always possible—or strategic. In these moments, confronting the challenge directly isn't just the best course of action; it's the only one that can lead to real change.

Avoidance might offer temporary relief, but it allows the problem to fester and grow, ultimately making it harder to address. Confronting the issue now—while you still have some control—puts the power back in your hands.

Key Insight: Delaying the inevitable isn't a strategy; it's a gamble you're likely to lose. By facing the challenge head-on, you take control of the narrative and prevent things from spiraling further out of hand. When there's no way out, the best move is forward.

For instance:

- **Living Under Surveillance:** You're being monitored by the regime and can't leave without drawing suspicion. Activists in countries like

178

North Korea or Iran often have no choice but to organize covertly within their own borders.

- **Forced Conscription or Crackdowns:** People in conflict zones, like Ukrainian civilians during the Russian invasion, have had to defend their homes because there was no safe escape route.

- **State Control of Resources:** When a regime blocks access to basic necessities—like in Venezuela during the economic collapse—resistance means organizing locally to survive and push back.

Loujain al-Hathloul, the Woman Who Said, "Not Today, Patriarchy"

What do you do when your entire country tells you that you're less than, that you need permission to live your life? If you're Loujain al-Hathloul, you say, "Watch me," and then you break every rule they throw at you.

180

Women weren't allowed behind the wheel because, heaven forbid, they might think for themselves. Loujain wasn't having it.

What a Girl's Gotta Know

The next time someone tells you, "You can't," channel your inner Loujain and show them exactly why you can.

Meet Loujain: A Force to Be Reckoned With

Born in 1989 in Saudi Arabia, Loujain al-Hathloul didn't set out to be a rebel. But living in a country where women couldn't drive, travel freely, or make basic decisions without a man's say-so will light a fire in anyone. And Loujain? She didn't just sit around fuming—she got to work.

In 2013, she started calling out the kingdom's misogynistic laws, particularly the infamous driving ban on women. It wasn't just about cars; it was about freedom. Women weren't allowed behind the wheel because, heaven forbid, they might *think for themselves.* Loujain wasn't having it.

The First Rule She Broke

Fast forward to 2014. Loujain decided to take a little road trip—nothing crazy, just driving herself from the UAE to Saudi Arabia. It was a bold, defiant move that screamed, "This law is ridiculous, and I'm going to show you just how much." Naturally, the authorities flipped out. She was arrested, interrogated, and detained. But did that stop her? Absolutely not.

Fighting the Big Fight

Loujain wasn't just about driving. She also went after the male guardianship system—a deeply oppressive set of laws that basically said every woman needed a man's permission to exist. Want to travel? Ask your dad. Want to get married? Better have your brother's OK. Loujain said, "Enough."

Her activism gained global attention, and while many applauded her bravery, Saudi authorities were not among them. They ac-

182

cused her of "destabilizing the kingdom." (Translation: She was scaring them by calling out their BS.)

The Crackdown

In 2018, just weeks before Saudi Arabia lifted the driving ban (because, spoiler alert, activists like Loujain made it impossible to ignore), she was arrested again. This time, they hit her with everything they had: imprisonment, torture, and charges so vague they could mean anything.

She spent nearly three years in prison, enduring horrors most of us can't imagine. And when she was finally released in February 2021, it came with conditions: a travel ban, probation, and constant monitoring. The regime might have thought they'd silenced her. Spoiler alert: They hadn't.

Why Loujain's Story Matters

Loujain didn't back down, not even when the stakes were impossibly high. She knew what was right, and she fought for it with everything she had. Her courage forced change—a driving ban that's no longer, a guardianship system under global scrutiny—and inspired a new generation of women to stand up and demand more.

Fascism, patriarchy, oppression—they rely on fear to keep people quiet. Loujain al-Hathloul is proof that one voice, no matter how much the system tries to silence it, can roar loud enough to shake the world. So the next time someone tells you, "You can't," channel your inner Loujain and show them exactly why you can.

Prepare for the Fight You Can't Avoid

Having the advantage doesn't guarantee victory, but it gives you a fighting chance. When you're better prepared, better connected, and better informed, you can turn the tide against even the most oppressive regimes. Dictators are strong only as long as they appear invincible—your advantage is showing the cracks in their armor and rallying others to help widen them.

Stand firm, fight smart, and keep your eyes on the goal.

Checklist for the battle ahead

Gather Evidence: Dictators thrive on controlling narratives. Document abuses, corruption, and any cracks in the regime's foundation. The truth is your most powerful weapon.

Example: Video footage, leaked documents, or testimony from witnesses can rally public opinion and international allies.

184

☐ **Build Your Network:** Resistance isn't a solo act. Strengthen your connections with like-minded activists, community leaders, and even sympathetic insiders. Collaborate with international organizations for funding, asylum options, or amplification of your cause.

☐ **Understand Your Opponent:** Study the dictator's playbook. Where are their weaknesses? What do they fear most—public dissent, financial sanctions, international scrutiny? Plan your moves to exploit those vulnerabilities.

☐ **Stay Agile:** Even with the upper hand, dictatorships are unpredictable. Be ready to adapt your tactics, change your location, or shift your focus as the fight evolves.

Preparing mentally

Acknowledge the Reality: Accept that there's no escaping this situation. Denial wastes time and energy you could use to prepare.

Mindset Shift: This isn't about waiting for rescue; it's about becoming your own hero.

Learn from Others: Look to historical and contemporary examples of people who've faced similar challenges.

185

From resistance movements in occupied France during WWII to modern pro-democracy protests in Myanmar, there's a blueprint for survival and action. *Pro Tip:* Study how others navigated impossible situations and adapted their strategies when circumstances changed.

Prepare for Retaliation: Dictators and oppressive systems often respond harshly to dissent. Have contingency plans in place for your safety and the safety of those around you.

Examples: Identify safe houses, create encrypted communication channels, and memorize key contacts and escape routes.

Blueprint for Resistance: Lessons from Myanmar

The pro-democracy resistance in Myanmar offers a modern playbook for surviving and pushing back against an oppressive regime. Following the military coup in 2021, ordinary citizens, activists, and workers banded together to fight for their freedom, demonstrating resilience, creativity, and courage. Here's how they did it:

Underground Organization

Faced with violent crackdowns, activists formed decentralized networks to coordinate protests, strikes, and civil disobedience. Using encrypted messaging apps like Signal and Telegram, they kept communication secure while maintaining anonymity to avoid government surveillance.

Resourcefulness

With access to resources limited by military control, protesters relied on ingenuity:

- Crafted homemade protective gear like shields and helmets to defend against police violence.

187

- Built barricades from scrap materials to block security forces during demonstrations.

- Used VPNs and other tools to bypass internet blackouts and share information with the world.

Civil Disobedience

One of the most effective tools of the Myanmar resistance was the *Civil Disobedience Movement (CDM):*

- Workers in critical sectors like transportation, healthcare, and banking went on strike, crippling the regime's ability to govern effectively.

- Students, teachers, and professionals joined en masse, creating a unified front that highlighted the widespread rejection of military rule.

Propaganda and Messaging

Despite the military's attempts to suppress information, activists found ways to amplify their message:

- Documented human rights abuses through photos and videos, often at great personal risk, to share with international media.

- Used social media platforms like Twitter and Face-

188

book to rally global awareness and support.

- Adopted the **three-finger salute**—a symbol of resistance borrowed from *The Hunger Games*—as a unifying emblem for their movement.

External Support

Activists sought solidarity and aid from the international community:

- Garnered attention from human rights organizations and global governments, leading to sanctions and condemnation of the military junta.

- Advocated for international pressure to restrict the military's access to funding and weapons.

Adaptability and Resilience

The movement continually evolved its tactics in response to the regime's brutality:

- When large-scale protests became too dangerous, activists turned to flash mob demonstrations, dispersing quickly to evade arrests.

- Resistance moved into rural areas, with some forming *People's Defense Forces (PDFs)* to engage in

189

guerilla warfare against the military.

Symbolism and Solidarity

Symbols became a rallying point for unity and hope:

- The three-finger salute and the wearing of red ribbons became widely recognized emblems of the fight for democracy.
- Public acts of resistance, like banging pots and pans to ward off evil spirits (a traditional practice), became a nightly protest ritual, reminding everyone that the fight continued.

Why It Matters

The Myanmar resistance shows that even against a heavily armed and oppressive regime, people can find ways to organize, resist, and fight back. Their strategies—decentralized organization, civil disobedience, and creative adaptation—offer a powerful blueprint for others facing authoritarianism. The fight is ongoing, but their bravery and resilience have already proven that resistance is possible, even in the darkest of times.

190

Section 2: Escape, Evade, Survive: Getting Out or Staying Hidden

There comes a moment when staying and fighting isn't just unwise—it's downright impossible. Maybe the walls are closing in, the risks are too high, or the resistance needs a fresh start from a safer place. Whatever the reason, knowing when it's time to run can mean the difference between surviving to fight another day or becoming another cautionary tale.

But let's be clear: running isn't giving up. It's a strategic move—a calculated retreat to regroup, rethink, and strike back when the odds are in your favor. From escaping surveillance to crossing borders, blending into the crowd, or setting up a base of operations far from the dictator's reach, running is about preserving your life and your mission. Survival hinges on preparation, adaptability, and the ability to move or blend as circumstances demand.

Crossing Borders: How to Escape When You Have To

When it's time to go, it's time to go. Crossing borders to escape a hostile regime is high-risk, but sometimes it's the only option. Preparation is your best weapon, so let's talk about how to make your exit smooth, stealthy, and successful.

Know Your Exit Points

Not all borders are created equal. Some are crawling with guards who'll ask too many questions, and some have corruption baked into the process. Research the safest spots to cross—ones with minimal oversight or a reputation for being manageable. If official checkpoints are a no-go, look for unofficial routes, like forest trails or backroads used by others in similar situations.

Pro Tip: Ask around or check online refugee forums for updated info—what worked yesterday might not work today.

Prepare Essential Documents

Your papers are everything. Keep your ID, passport, and visas (if you need them) somewhere easy to grab but hard to spot—hidden pockets and discreet pouches are your new best friends. Digital backups? Non-negotiable. Upload encrypted copies of everything to a secure cloud service so you're not stranded if you lose the originals.

Bonus Hack: If your regime loves random searches, make fake versions of less critical documents as decoys.

193

Travel Light and Blend In

No one should look at you and think, "There's someone fleeing the country." Wear low-key clothes that blend with the locals, and carry a small bag with just the essentials—this isn't the time for overpacking. Hide cash or valuables in creative spots like your shoes or sewn into your clothes. The goal? Look like someone heading to a casual lunch, not a high-stakes border dash.

Seek Assistance if Possible

Don't go it alone if you don't have to. Refugee support organizations, underground networks, or even a friend of a friend can help smooth the way. These people are often pros at navigating tricky crossings and might provide shelter, transport, or legal advice. If you've got contacts on the other side, loop them in—they can be a lifeline when you arrive.

Quick Reality Check: Not everyone offering help is trustworthy. Vet your sources and trust your gut.

Stay Alert and Flexible

Plans? Amazing. Backup plans? Even better. Border situations can change fast—guards swap shifts, routes close, and new dangers pop up out of nowhere. Keep your cool and be ready to pivot. Stick to cash for transactions so you don't leave a digital breadcrumb trail, and always, *always* pay attention to your surroundings. Your gut feeling? Trust it—it's usually right.

Crossing borders isn't glamorous or easy, but it's survivable with the right prep and mindset. Think ahead, stay sharp, and remember: getting out is just the beginning. Once you're safe, you'll have what you need to keep fighting for a better future—because no regime gets to have the last word.

Hiding in Plain Sight: The Art of Disappearing Without Leaving

When escape isn't possible, survival depends on staying under the radar while continuing to resist in subtle ways. Here's how to make yourself less visible to those who might target you while keeping your mission alive.

Alter Your Routine

Predictability is dangerous. If someone knows where you'll be or what you'll do at any given time, you become an easy target. Start by shaking up your daily habits.

- Avoid visiting the same places at the same times every day. For example, if you usually stop by the same café for breakfast or take the same route to work, change it up.

- Use different modes of transportation. Alternate between buses, trains, bikes, or walking if possible, and avoid sticking to a single route.

By becoming less predictable, you make it harder for

anyone to track your movements or anticipate your next steps.

Adopt a New Persona

Sometimes, staying safe means blending in. If you're being watched, small changes to your appearance and habits can make a big difference.

- Simplify your online presence by scrubbing social media profiles and removing any identifiable information that could connect you to dissent or activism.

- Consider subtle physical changes, like altering your hairstyle, growing facial hair, or wearing glasses (real or fake). Adjusting your clothing style to align with the local majority can help you avoid standing out.

The goal isn't to completely reinvent yourself, but to become less recognizable and more difficult to associate with your former identity.

Lay Low on Social Media

Social media can be a double-edged sword in a high-risk situation. While it's tempting to keep posting updates or share your experiences, doing so can give away your location or put others at risk.

197

- Avoid posting real-time updates or tagging your location. Sharing even seemingly innocent details, like a photo of a landmark or a meal, can reveal more than you realize.

- Use encrypted communication tools and aliases if you must communicate with others online. Apps like Signal or Proton-Mail can help protect your privacy and keep your conversations secure.

Remember, silence online doesn't mean you're giving up—it's a strategic pause to protect yourself and your mission.

Build Local Allies

Even when you're lying low, you don't have to do it alone. Quietly building relationships with trusted individuals in your community can provide critical support.

- Establish connections with people who can provide cover, resources, or warnings if danger arises. These might include neighbors, shopkeepers, or even sympathetic strangers.

- Find ways to integrate into the community without drawing undue attention. Participate in local activities or volunteer quietly, but avoid becoming the center of attention.

Allies on the ground can provide you with information, supplies, or even an escape route when you need it most.

Stay Quiet, Stay Calm

When tensions are high, it's easy to act on emotion—but staying calm and quiet is your best defense. Avoid behaviors that might draw attention or escalate the situation.

- Avoid confrontations, loud arguments, or making public statements about your dissent. Even a careless word in the wrong place could lead to scrutiny.

- Appear compliant on the surface while continuing to resist covertly. Whether it's attending government-mandated events or following local dress codes, blending in can keep you safe while you plan your next move.

Remaining calm and collected, even in tense situations, allows you to maintain control and avoid unnecessary risks.

Hiding in plain sight isn't about losing yourself—it's about protecting yourself while finding new ways to keep fighting. By adapting your routines, appearance, and behavior, you can outmaneuver those who seek to control you and continue to work toward freedom.

Creating a Plan B (C, D & E): Always Be Ready

Let's face it: Plan A is a dream. It's the "everything goes perfectly" scenario, and spoiler alert—it almost never does. When you're up against fascists, dictators, or any oppressive system, you need a backup plan—or five. Having Plans B, C, D, and E means you'll never be caught flat-footed. If they close one door, you'll already know how to kick down another. Here's how to make sure you're always one step ahead.

Map Out Scenarios

You can't predict the future, but you **can** prepare for its nasty surprises. What happens if you get stopped at a checkpoint? What if your escape route is blown? What if your supplies run out halfway to safety?

- Think through the possibilities—yes, even the worst ones—and plan immediate steps and long-term solutions for each.

- If Plan A fails, what's your Plan B? And if that fails, what's next? Keep layering contingencies so you're never left stranded.

200

- Remember: hope is not a strategy. Preparation is.

Secure Resources

The best-laid plans won't matter if you're empty-handed when it's go-time. Stock up and stash smart.

- Hide essentials—cash, food, medicine—in places you can access quickly. Split them across multiple spots so one loss doesn't ruin you. (**Pro tip:** A few rolled-up bills in your bra? Classic.)

- Pack a "go-bag" that's light but loaded. Think: first aid kit, portable charger, flashlight, water purification tablets, and snacks that won't expire. Oh, and a pair of comfy shoes—you might be walking more than you'd like.

Create a Network

Even lone wolves need a pack sometimes. Building a reliable network isn't just smart; it's essential.

- Make connections with people who can offer help, shelter, or a warning when danger's near. Neighbors, co-workers, the nice lady at the market—anyone you trust enough to have your back.

- Use multiple ways to stay in touch. If one line goes dark, you'll need another. Stick to encrypted apps like Signal, and maybe develop a few secret hand signals for good measure.

Learn Basic Survival Skills

We're not saying you need to become Jason Bourne, but knowing a few key skills can keep you alive when things go sideways.

- Learn to navigate without Google Maps. A paper map and compass can be lifesavers, especially if your phone goes dead.

- Basic first aid isn't optional—know how to treat cuts, stop bleeding, and deal with dehydration.

- If things get hairy, self-defense moves can give you the edge. And hey, if you can use pepper spray, you're already halfway there.

If you end up off the grid, knowing how to find water, forage for food, or build shelter could mean the difference between survival and "well, that's unfortunate."

Prepare for Re-entry

Sometimes, you'll need to go back or stay under the radar where you already are. Don't just waltz back in like it's no big deal—prepare.

- Before re-entering, check in with your network. Is it safe? Are there eyes on you? If there's even a whiff of danger, rethink your approach.

- When you return, blend in like a pro. New haircut, different clothes, different habits. Avoid your old stomping grounds, at least for a while, and don't make contact with people who might be under surveillance.

Your goal is to slide back in unnoticed, not to announce, "Guess who's back?"

Final Thought

Backup plans aren't just smart—they're survival. Having multiple options means you're never out of moves, no matter how bad things get. Whether it's a hidden stash of cash, a network of allies, or a Plan Z you hope you never need, preparation is power. You can't control the chaos, but you can make sure you're ready to face it head-on—and win.

Change Starts Somewhere, Why Not with You?

What American Women Can Learn from the 4B Movement and Liberia's Women of Peace

Oppression takes many forms, whether it's systemic patriarchy, racial inequality, or economic injustice. While the struggles of American women are shaped by a unique cultural and political landscape, movements like South Korea's 4B Movement and Liberia's Women of Peace offer valuable lessons in resilience, unity, and the power of collective action. Here's how American women can draw inspiration from these global examples:

1. Build Unity Across Differences

- *What We Can Learn:* The Women of Liberia Mass Action for Peace succeeded because they united across religious and cultural divides. Christians and Muslims, young and old, came together with a shared goal: peace. This unity was more powerful than any one faction could have achieved alone.

- *Application in America:* In the U.S., building coalitions across race, class, and political ideology is essential for combating systemic issues like reproductive rights rollbacks, workplace discrimination, and violence against women. Women must focus on common goals rather than divisive differences.

2. Challenge Cultural Norms

- *What We Can Learn:* The 4B Movement defies deeply entrenched societal expectations by rejecting marriage, motherhood, and even relationships with men. This radical reimagining of what it means to be a woman is a powerful act of resistance.

- *Application in America:* American women can challenge

205

outdated norms that tie their worth to their marital status, caregiving roles, or appearance. By embracing alternative life paths—whether singlehood, child-free living, or prioritizing personal fulfillment—they can push back against a culture that limits women's choices.

3. Use Nonviolent Resistance

- *What We Can Learn:* Both movements leaned heavily on nonviolent tactics. Liberian women staged sit-ins, protests, and even threatened to strip naked to shame negotiators into action. The 4B Movement uses peaceful disengagement by simply opting out of patriarchal systems.

- *Application in America:* Nonviolent resistance, such as boycotts, marches, and civil disobedience, has long been effective in U.S. social movements. American women can leverage these tactics to fight injustices like wage gaps, sexual harassment, and restrictive laws.

4. Prioritize Grassroots Activism

- *What We Can Learn:* Both movements started small—groups

of women coming together, sharing their frustrations, and deciding to act. The power came from their grassroots nature, making their movements accessible and relatable.

- *Application in America:* American women can replicate this by forming local coalitions, whether it's neighborhood groups advocating for reproductive healthcare or online networks pushing for better workplace policies. Change often begins in small, committed groups.

---

5. **Reclaim Autonomy**

- *What We Can Learn:* The 4B Movement empowers women by encouraging them to step away from systems that exploit or devalue them. The Liberian women reclaimed agency in the peace process, forcing powerful men to listen and act.

- *Application in America:* American women can take control of their narratives, from financial independence to political representation. Whether it's starting businesses, running for office, or redefining success on their terms, reclaiming autonomy is a key step toward equality.

207

6. **Leverage the Power of Persistence**

- *What We Can Learn:* Neither movement achieved success overnight. Liberian women protested daily under the hot sun for months. Members of the 4B Movement face constant societal pressure to conform but remain steadfast.

- *Application in America:* Persistence is critical in the face of setbacks. Progress, especially on issues like equal pay, reproductive rights, or gender-based violence, requires a long-term commitment to advocacy and activism.

208

STORYTIME

How a Group of Women Stopped a War

Okay, picture this: Liberia, early 2000s. The country is in chaos after years of civil war—brutal violence, families torn apart, and women bearing the worst of it. Life was a nightmare.

Leymah Gbowee

A social worker who decided, "Enough is enough." She had a dream (literally) where women came together to pray for peace. So, she made it happen. She gathered women—Christian, Muslim, whoever—and started a movement: *Women of Liberia Mass Action for Peace.*

209

When women unite, we're unstoppable. Whether it's peace, progress, or justice, we get it done.

The Moment That Changed Everything

When peace talks in Ghana stalled (because the men in charge were busy arguing), these women traveled there and blocked the delegates inside. They refused to move until a deal was made. Security tried to remove them, and Leymah said, "Touch us, and I'll strip naked." (In Liberian culture, that's a big deal—a serious act of shame.) Spoiler: they didn't touch her.

Guess what? The men caved. A peace agreement was signed, and the war finally ended.

What Happened Next?

In 2005, Liberia elected **Ellen Johnson Sirleaf,** Africa's first female president. The women had fought for peace—and they didn't stop until they got real change.

The Lesson?

When women unite, they're unstoppable. Whether it's peace, progress, or justice, we get it done. Leymah and her crew didn't have money or power, just courage and the will to act. So, next time you think, "What can I do?" remember them. Change starts somewhere—and it can start with you.

211

4B: Redefining Womanhood in South Korea

The *4B Movement* originated in South Korea as a feminist and anti-patriarchy movement advocating for women's independence and challenging traditional gender roles. The name "4B" stands for "Four Nos" (in Korean)—a rejection of **marriage**, **childbirth**, **dating**, and **sexual relationships** with men. This movement is closely tied to a broader critique of the patriarchy, misogyny, and the cultural expectations placed on women in South Korea.

212

The movement arose in response to deep-rooted societal issues in South Korea, such as:

1. *Rampant Gender Inequality:* South Korea has one of the largest gender pay gaps in the world, and women face significant challenges balancing work and family life.

2. *Misogyny and Femicide:* High-profile cases of violence against women and widespread online harassment brought attention to the systemic dangers women face.

3. *"Hell Joseon" Pressures:* The term describes the intense societal pressure to conform, including expectations for women to marry, have children, and uphold patriarchal family structures.

4. *Digital Sex Crimes:* Incidents involving spy cameras ("molka") and the online spread of non-consensual intimate videos have heightened fears and mistrust of men.

Core Principles of 4B

The 4B movement encourages women to reject societal norms that perpetuate dependence on men and instead focus on their own well-being, careers, and freedom. The "Four Nos" stand for:

213

1. *No Marriage:* Rejecting traditional marriage, where women often bear unequal burdens of domestic work and childcare.

2. *No Childbirth:* Refusing to have children, challenging the cultural expectation that women must sacrifice their careers and personal goals for motherhood.

3. *No Dating:* Avoiding romantic relationships with men, often due to distrust and the belief that they perpetuate patriarchal dynamics.

4. *No Sexual Relationships with Men:* This stance includes celibacy or seeking alternative forms of sexuality, promoting autonomy over their bodies.

Who Are the Members?

The movement appeals to young women, particularly millennials and Gen Z, who feel trapped by traditional gender roles and economic precarity. Many 4B participants identify as "radical feminists," and some embrace singlehood or non-heteronormative lifestyles.

Impact of the 4B Movement

1. **Challenging Patriarchal Norms:**
   The movement confronts deeply ingrained cultural and societal expectations, particularly those that tie a woman's value to her relationship with men.

2. **Declining Birth Rates:**
   South Korea already has one of the world's lowest fertility rates, and the 4B movement has sparked debates about the long-term effects of women opting out of marriage and childbirth.

3. **Feminist Discourse:**
   The movement has amplified discussions around feminism, equality, and women's rights in South Korea, inspiring women globally to question patriarchal structures.

4. **Criticism and Backlash:**
   The movement has faced backlash from conservative groups and men's rights activists, who accuse 4B members of "man-hating." Some critics argue it could

215

exacerbate societal issues like the aging population and labor shortages.

Global Relevance

While the 4B movement is uniquely Korean in its context, its principles resonate with feminist movements worldwide that call for autonomy, equality, and the rejection of oppressive norms. It serves as a powerful reminder that women can redefine their roles in society on their own terms.

A Call to Action

The challenges American women face—whether systemic sexism, racial disparities, or threats to bodily autonomy—can seem overwhelming. But movements like the 4B Movement and the Women of Liberia Mass Action for Peace show that change is possible when women come together, challenge the status quo, and refuse to back down.

These global lessons remind us that progress doesn't come from waiting for permission—it comes from creating the change we want to see. In the face of oppression, American women can find strength in solidarity, inspiration in persistence, and empowerment in their own voices.

217